OHIO SPORTS TRIVIA

Vince Guerrieri
and
J. Alexander Poulton

OVER
TIME
BOOKS

The Publisher: OverTime Books is an imprint of Éditions de la Montagne
Verte

Library and Archives Canada Cataloguing in Publication

Guerrieri, Vince, 1977–
          Ohio sports trivia / Vince Guerrieri, J. Alexander Poulton.

Includes bibliographical references.
ISBN 978-1-897277-65-2

          1. Sports—Ohio—Miscellanea. I. Poulton, J. Alexander (Jay
Alexander), 1977– II. Title.

GV584.O3G83 2011 796.09771   C2011-901463-7

Project Director: J. Alexander Poulton
Editor: Sheila Quinlan
Cover Images: baseball glove, © Bobbiholmes | Dreamstime.com; football,
© Toddtaulman | Dreamstime.com; track sprinter, © Jupiterimages;
boxing gloves, © Zedcor Wholly Owned; golfer, © iStockphoto.com
| Sergey Kashkin; basketball hoop, © 2011 Thinkstock; race car,
© Lawrence Weslowski Jr | Dreamstime.com; fishing lure, © Alexey
Kaznin | Hemera | Thinkstock; dry fly fishing lure, © 2011 iStockphoto
| Thinkstock; Cleveland Browns Stadium, home of the Cleveland
Browns, © 2011 Grigor Atanasov | Dreamstime.com; Great American
Ball Park Park, home of the Cincinnati Reds, © 2011 Ffooter
| Dreamstime.com; all other photos, © Photos.com

We acknowledge the financial support of the Government of Canada
through the Canada Book Fund (CBF) for our publishing activities.

Government of Québec—Tax Credit for book publishing—Adminstered
by SODEC

 Canadian   Patrimoine   **SODEC**
Heritage   canadien   Québec

PC: 5

Contents

Introduction 7

Chapter 1:
Football in the Buckeye State 10

Chapter 2:
**Baseball: From Cy Young to Pete Rose,
and Beyond** 67

Chapter 3:
Hockey: The NCAA, the AHL and the NHL 125

Chapter 4:
**Basketball: High School Phenoms, College
Legends, a King and a Big O.** 139

Chapter 5:
**Boxing: Ohio Practitioners of the
Sweet Science** 167

Chapter 6:
Golf: Hitting the Links in Ohio 178

Chapter 7:
**Potpourri: Pool, Fishing and the "Gravity
Grand Prix"** 184

Chapter 8:
**Ohio Individuals: Immortals and Less
Well-known Greats** 196

Chapter 9:
Ohio Hall of Famers 209

Notes on Sources 219

Dedication

To R.A.B.

–Jay Poulton

To my father, whose words of wisdom to me
include, "Stay between your guy and the hoop."

–Vince Guerrieri

Acknowledgments

When I was in first grade, my elementary school principal, Mr. Winsen, asked me if I read the newspaper. I said only the comics. "Read the sports section," he told me, setting me on my career path, which has, at various times, included reading the sports section before it goes to print.

My mother, who is sports literate only in the functional sense, helped me acquire many of the books in my sports reference library. The rest came from the local library. Most public libraries in Ohio have seen severe cutbacks in state funding and are either trying to find alternative revenue sources (passing levies) or making corresponding reductions in service. Please support your local library.

A lot of the research came from *Sports Illustrated*, which has chronicled sport since 1954. I owe a tremendous debt of gratitude to whoever decided to put all of their archives online. That magazine is a wealth of resources, and a treasure trove for anyone who likes reading good writing about sports.

I'd also like to thank two of my friends: Zach Baker and Ryan Crincic. Both perused early drafts of this book and offered their helpful hints. Zach, like me, is a sports nut who happened to find a way to make a living from it; and the sports knowledge and analysis Crin can pull from memory dwarfs even my own.

And last but not least, I'd like to thank my wife Shannon for her enduring patience on days where I would disappear into our office at home to write this book.

–Vince Guerrieri

Introduction

Through a series of minor miracles (OK, I asked for a media pass, and the Detroit Tigers said yes), I ended up on the field for the last Opening Day at Tiger Stadium in 1999.

Gene Budig, the president of the American League, was giving interviews. Alan Trammell, a coach for the Tigers, was standing on the dugout steps signing autographs. I was standing on the field on grass trod by every American League player—and more than a few National League players—from Ty Cobb to Ken Griffey Jr. It was an awe-inspiring moment for me, and one of the first times in my life that I had one of those moments.

Having lived in Ohio, I should have had more. There is a rich tradition of history throughout the state. It's called the "Mother of Presidents" because it can claim eight presidents as natives. The odyssey of Morgan's Raiders in the Civil War ended in Columbiana County, not far from the place where Pretty Boy Floyd met his end 70 years later. Johnson's Island in northwestern Ohio was home to a Confederate prisoner of war camp during the

Civil War, and Fort Meigs outside of Toledo was an important point in the western front of the War of 1812.

And this rich history extends to sports. The namesakes of both the Cy Young Award and the Heisman Trophy hail from Ohio. Miami University in the southwestern corner of the state calls itself the "Cradle of Coaches," and rightly so. Both Cleveland and Cincinnati have their place in the annals of sports. Columbus has Ohio State and its own sports history. And there are many, many other great moments and historic events that took place throughout the state—from small cities such as Youngstown and Springfield to small towns such as LaRue and Portsmouth.

Without even knowing, people could be treading on historic ground. As a child, my grandmother played in the Hupmobile dealership in Canton where the NFL was born. I played pee-wee football on the same field where the first penalty flag was thrown, and I and countless others walked across the campus of Bowling Green State University at the same spot where Lou Groza practiced field goals and Otto Graham handed the ball off to Marion Motley.

This book was a labor of love. Drawing from my extensive library of sports books and my research as a newspaper reporter, I had a broad base of Ohio sports knowledge. But this book was a learning experience even for me. There were things I was shocked to find out.

This is not a comprehensive book of Ohio sports history—nor is it intended to be. Rather, it's meant to offer a taste of the great athletes in and from Ohio, and of the sporting history that was made here. I hope there are things in this book that will lead even the most hardcore sports fan to say, "Huh. I didn't know that!" But above all, I hope you enjoy reading it as much as I enjoyed writing it.

Chapter 1

Football in the Buckeye State

In a sports-mad state like Ohio, football seems to take primary—and nearly primal—importance. The Buckeye State seems to stop on a dime when its namesake football team plays on Saturday afternoons, and the National Football League started in Canton but took root in cities throughout Ohio. High school teams play rivalry grudge matches dating back more than a century. Overall, no state can claim more of a role in the development of football and as many of its success stories as can Ohio.

Professional Football

Origins of the NFL

Professional football—that is to say, the idea of paying people to play football—dates back to 1892, when Pudge Heffelfinger was paid $500 to play for the Allegheny Athletic Association. A "National Football League" of teams in Pittsburgh and Philadelphia was formed in 1903, but the origins of what we now know as the NFL go back to September 17, 1920, when a group of 11 men met in a Hupmobile dealership owned by Ralph Hay on Cleveland Avenue in Canton. Hay owned the Canton Bulldogs, and the other 10 men represented other football clubs: the Decatur Staleys (which went on to become the Chicago Bears), the Chicago Cardinals, the Akron Pros, the Cleveland Indians, the Dayton Triangles, the Massillon Tigers, the Hammond Pros, the Muncie Flyers, the Rock Island Independents and the Rochester (New York) Jeffersons.

Hay brought with him one of his players, who also happened to be a coach and one of the most famous athletes of all time: Jim Thorpe. Hay was asked to become president of the league, but he declined. Realizing his name was relatively obscure and looking for someone with more star power, he suggested Thorpe. Stanley Cofall of the Cleveland team became vice president, and Art Ranney of the Akron team became secretary-treasurer. League membership was set at $100. (At the time, a new Ford Model T cost $310.)

The Canton newspapers relegated the story of the new circuit to inside the sports section. The front page news was that the Bulldogs had signed Wilbur Henry, a Mansfield native who played college football at Washington & Jefferson. Henry went on to become one of the charter inductees of the Pro Football Hall of Fame—when it opened in Canton in 1963.

That fall of 1920, 10 of the 11 teams that met at Hay's dealership played football under the auspices of the American Professional Football Association (APFA). Massillon didn't field a team that year.

The Detroit Heralds, Columbus Panhandles and Chicago Tigers are regarded as charter members of the league, having scheduled several APFA teams during the year. In fact, the Panhandles were the visiting team for what is now regarded as the first NFL game, on October 3, 1920, in Howell Field at Triangle Park in Dayton. The Triangles won, 14–0. An Ohio Historic Marker now commemorates the spot.

The Akron Pros were the first champions, going 8–0–3 in the circuit.

The Oorang Indians

Today, the smallest city with an NFL team—the smallest city with any major league sports team—is Green Bay, Wisconsin. The entire population of the city—around 102,000—could fit in Cowboys Stadium, where the Packers won Super Bowl XLV. But the smallest city ever to have an NFL franchise is tiny LaRue, in Marion County, Ohio. The community was home to a unique franchise, the Oorang Indians. But the team never played a game in LaRue. They had one home game, but they played it in Marion.

Like many franchises of the day (the Packers were so named because they were sponsored by a Chicago-area meat-packing company), the Oorang Indians were named for the business of their owner, Walter Lingo, who was a breeder of Airedales. Lingo created the King Oorang

Airedales, which he called the world's great all-around dogs.

To get further publicity, he bought into the NFL and created the Oorang Indians. The dogs he bred cost $150 each. The entry fee to join the NFL was $100. Jim Thorpe was one of Lingo's celebrity endorsers for the Oorang Kennels, and Lingo lured him into running a football team comprised entirely of American Indians.

The Oorang Indians were used by Lingo as a barnstorming team, playing across the country to drum up publicity for the Oorang Kennels. Players worked in the kennels and paraded the dogs around before the game and at halftime. Some of the players also performed at halftime, throwing tomahawks and doing Indian dances. One player wrestled a bear at halftime, leading some people to credit Lingo with the invention of the halftime show.

The Indians won a total of four games in two years, and after the first year of their existence, the novelty wore off. They disbanded after the 1923 season, but tiny LaRue remains the smallest city ever to have boasted an NFL team.

Ongoing Rivalry

The pro teams in Massillon and Canton led to one more platform for what might be the most bruising gridiron rivalry in Ohio. The pro teams were indeed rivals, but the cities have become inseparable in national lore for their high school football rivalry between Massillon Washington and Canton McKinley.

It's the oldest high school rivalry in the state, with 120 meetings going back to 1894. As of this writing, Massillon has a 64–51–5 edge. Massillon's nickname, the Tigers, comes from the city's former professional team, and it would go on to inspire the name of another professional football team.

McKinley football plays its home games at Fawcett Stadium. That stadium is also the site of the NFL Hall of Fame game. The high school is next to the stadium, which is right behind the Pro Football Hall of Fame. Timken High School and Walsh and Malone colleges also play at Fawcett Stadium, and, along with Paul Brown Tiger Stadium in Massillon, it hosts the Ohio high school football championships.

Paul Brown Tiger Stadium was built with Works Progress Administration (WPA) money, $150,000 from the federal government and $96,000 from the Massillon school board. At the same time, the WPA contributed $400,000 to the construction of Fawcett Stadium. The school district floated a $100,000 bond issue to pay for the rest. Fawcett Stadium opened in 1939 with a capacity of more than 15,000 (it currently seats more than 22,000). Tiger Stadium also opened in 1939, seating more than 21,000. In 1976, the stadium was renamed to honor Brown, a former Massillon football coach and arguably the most influential figure in the game of football.

Paul Brown

Paul Eugene Brown was born September 7, 1908, in Norwalk, a small town in northern Ohio almost halfway between Cleveland and Toledo. His father worked for the Wheeling and Lake Erie Railway and was transferred to Massillon when Paul was nine. In high school, Paul played football for the Tigers—alongside Harry Stuhldreher, who went on to become one of the Four Horsemen of Notre Dame (Irish halfback Don Miller was also an Ohio native, from Defiance).

After high school, Brown went to Ohio State for a year but ended up transferring to Miami of Ohio in Oxford. He started at quarterback for two years for the Redskins, and although he was eligible for a Rhodes scholarship, he got a teaching job at a prep school in Maryland.

In 1931, the Tigers went 1–9, and they reached out to Brown. In nine years, he went 80–8–2 as head coach, winning six state titles and four national titles (Ohio high school football didn't adopt a playoff system until 1972, so all the titles were, in the parlance of the time, "mythical," selected by sportswriters or by popular acclaim).

In 1940, Brown was hired as coach at Ohio State University. At the time, the Buckeyes head coaching job was known as a graveyard for coaches. However, in 1942, Brown coached the Ohio State team to its first national championship game, which it won. Brown went 18–8–1 with the Buckeyes before service in World War II beckoned. He was commissioned as a lieutenant junior grade and coached the Great Lakes Naval Station football team.

After coming home from World War II, Brown was hired as the first coach of the new All-American Football Conference (AAFC) team in Cleveland. The team was ultimately named the Browns, and under Brown's tutelage, obliterated the competition in the AAFC, winning all five league championships. In 1950, the Browns became one of the teams absorbed into the NFL, and they won three of the next six league championships—they were runners-up in the other three games. Brown went 157–63–8 in 17 seasons as coach of the Browns. He went on to start the Cincinnati Bengals in 1968, going 55–56–1 in eight seasons as coach before retiring in 1975.

Brown's innovations are concepts football fans and players now take for granted, including the use of playbooks, intelligence testing, reviewing of game film, messenger guards to bring plays to the offense, clocking players in the 40-yard dash and the first face masks in the NFL.

Brown's Coaching Tree

Paul Brown wasn't just a coach; he was also a cultivator of other coaches. His coaching tree extends for nearly half a century and includes some of the most successful NFL coaches in history.

Otto Graham, his prized quarterback in Cleveland, spent a year as the Washington Redskins coach before he was supplanted by Vince Lombardi in what turned out to be his final coaching job. Graham was also coach of the U.S. Coast Guard Academy for seven years.

Don Shula played for Brown in Cleveland before becoming head coach for the Baltimore Colts (who lost the NFL Championship game to the Browns in 1964—the last major championship won by a team in Cleveland) and the Miami Dolphins. Shula is the winningest coach in NFL history, with a total of 347 wins and two Super Bowl championships. He lost four other Super Bowls.

Shula's defensive coordinator in Baltimore was another former Brown, Chuck Noll, who spent 23 seasons as the Pittsburgh Steelers head coach. He is the only coach to win four Super Bowls.

Weeb Ewbank was an assistant for Brown before going on to win championships with the Colts and the New York Jets. Two of Ewbank's assistants were Buddy Ryan, the architect of the Chicago Bears' 46 defense and a head coach with the Philadelphia Eagles and Arizona Cardinals, and Chuck Knox, who coached the Seattle Seahawks, Buffalo Bills and Los Angeles Rams.

Lou Saban was a team captain for the Browns and went on to coach Boston, Buffalo and Denver in the American Football League. Saban's players in Buffalo included a young linebacker from the Pittsburgh area, Marty Schottenheimer, who would himself go on to be a successful coach.

The prodigal son in the Paul Brown coaching tree is Bill Walsh, who was an assistant for Brown with the Bengals. Walsh said that Brown actively worked against him getting a head coaching job in the NFL, and when Brown stepped down as Bengals coach in 1975, he passed over Walsh in favor of Bill "Tiger" Johnson. Walsh went on to greater glory as the head coach of the San Francisco 49ers, leading them to three Super Bowl championships in the 1980s—two of which came against the Bengals. It could be argued that Walsh's West Coast offense is an extension of the offenses Paul Brown was using.

In spite of Brown's lack of mentoring to Walsh—or because of it—Walsh begat many assistants who had great coaching careers, including Mike Holmgren, who has brought the Paul Brown coaching tree full circle, back to Cleveland, as has Ray Rhodes. Some other of Walsh's assistants who became head coaches include Tony Dungy (also a Chuck Noll acolyte), Dennis Green and Sam Wyche. They, in turn, have begat coaches Jon Gruden, Mike Shanahan, Jeff Fisher, Andy Reid and Mike Tomlin.

The Detroit Lions Start in...Ohio?

In 1929, the Portsmouth Spartans began play as an independent football team. The following year, the team joined what was by then the NFL, playing one of the first night games in the league, against the Brooklyn Dodgers—the relocated Dayton Triangles—at Universal Stadium. The Spartans went 5–6–3 in 1930; it was the only losing season the Spartans would have.

In 1931, the Spartans went 11–3, finishing one game behind the Green Bay Packers, who denied them a championship game bid. The Spartans turned around and beat the Packers in the 1932 regular season, 19–0. They went 6–2–4 in 1932 and finished tied for first place with the Bears. The Spartans and the Bears played in the first-ever playoff game in the NFL, which also turned out to be the first NFL game played indoors.

The game was scheduled to be played at Wrigley Field, but because of snow and sub-zero temperatures, an indoor venue had to be found. A 60-yard playing field, narrowed by 30 feet, was shoehorned into Chicago Stadium. The Bears prevailed 9–0, but the game led to several rule changes the following season: the goal posts were moved from the end line to the goal line, forward passes were now legal anywhere behind the line of scrimmage, and the NFL began to adopt its own rules, rather than using the collegiate rule book.

In 1933, the NFL split into two divisions, and the Spartans went 6–5, finishing a distant second in the Western Division to the Bears. The Spartans, then in the smallest city in the NFL, were floundering during the Great Depression. George "Dick" Richards, owner of WCX in Detroit, bought the Spartans and moved them to the Motor City, where they were renamed the Lions. Richards reasoned that the lion was the king of the jungle, so the new team would be so named to become the king of the NFL.

The NFL in Cleveland

The Cleveland Indians were part of the APFA when it was founded in 1920. Teams by the name of Indians, Bulldogs and Tigers came and went throughout the 1920s and early 1930s.

In 1936, a rival league to the NFL, the American Football League (AFL), was formed, including a team in Cleveland called the Rams. The Rams started play at League Park and played one year at Shaw High School Stadium in 1937 before playing in Municipal Stadium.

After that first year in the AFL, the team's owners bought into the NFL for $100,000. The group, headed by Homer Marshman, sold the team to Dan Reeves in 1941. The Rams were a middling-to-lousy team in the Western Division in their first six years, and in 1943, they suspended operations because of World War II.

Then in 1945, the Rams went 9–1 in the Western Division and hosted the Washington Redskins in the NFL Championship game at Municipal Stadium, on the shore of Lake Erie. Slingin' Sammy Baugh, the quarterback for the Redskins, threw a pass from his own end zone that hit the cross bar of the goal posts (which were on the goal line at the time). The pass caromed back and out of the end zone. The rules at the time made that a safety, which turned out to make the difference in the Rams' 15–14 win.

However, the Rams were awash in red ink. In four home games at League Park in 1945, they played to 73,000 fans, or less than capacity of Municipal Stadium at the time. The NFL Championship game was played before 32,000 fans. Reeves, who said he bought the team with the intention of moving it, asked NFL owners for permission to relocate to Los Angeles.

Reeves didn't want to compete with a team in a league that hadn't even played a down yet: the Cleveland Browns of the AAFC. It proved to be a wise move. In their opener in 1946, the Cleveland Browns drew more than 60,000 fans to watch them wax the Miami Seahawks, 44–0.

There was a new game in town.

The Birth of the Browns

In 1940, 52-year-old Arthur "Mickey" McBride had never been to a football game. That changed that fall, when his son enrolled at the University of Notre Dame. McBride made the drive from Cleveland to South Bend, Indiana, to watch the Irish. He was instantly smitten with the game and drove home to watch the Rams play.

McBride made his way in newspapers, serving as a circulation director when the title brought with it a certain amount of violence. He also owned the Yellow Cab Company in Cleveland, as well as owned and operated a horse racing wire service. He was a man who had accumulated a great deal of wealth, if not entirely inside the law. And now he wanted to buy a football team. McBride offered to buy the Rams from Dan Reeves in 1942, but he was turned down.

In 1944, Arch Ward, the sports editor of the *Chicago Tribune* and the man responsible for the creation of the Major League Baseball All-Star Game, was looking to create another football league, ideally one separate from the NFL, but the champion of each league would meet for a championship game—much like the Super Bowl when it started.

McBride was hooked for the Cleveland franchise. He wanted the best coach, the best players and the best promotions. He first wanted to pursue Notre Dame coach Frank Leahy but was dissuaded by the Notre Dame administration. McBride then asked a sportswriter for the *Plain Dealer* who the best football coach in America was.

"Paul Brown," came the response, almost reflexively.

So McBride hired him—and overpaid.

"I could have signed him for $15,000, but I wanted to make a big splash for publicity so I gave him $25,000," McBride said. "I wanted to say my team had the highest paid coach in America." Brown also received a stake in the ownership of the team. And then he went about assembling what was one of the best collections of talent in the country.

Assembling a Team

Paul Brown saw a lot of talent during his days coaching Massillon and Ohio State, and he drew from them when he was assembling the Browns. A total of seven players from Ohio State—including future Hall of Famers Lou Groza, Bill Willis and Dante Lavelli—were on his first roster in 1946, as was Marion Motley, a running back who played high school football at Canton McKinley, and former Tigers players Horace Gillom and Tommy James.

But the quarterback came from Illinois, a state crazy about basketball. Indeed, he played basketball in high school in Waukegan, and in college for Northwestern. All in all, he got eight letters in three sports: basketball, football and baseball. He was an All-American in football and basketball for the Wildcats, and he even played pro basketball for the Rochester Royals in the NBL—the forerunner to the NBA—winning the 1946 league championship.

He led the Wildcats to two wins in the three times they played Brown's Ohio State teams. He could throw. He could run. There was no doubt in Paul Brown's mind who would play quarterback for him: Otto Graham. It was a decision he wouldn't regret.

The Taxi Squad

Mickey McBride's ownership of the Browns allowed a new term to enter the pro football lexicon that remains today. McBride owned the Yellow Cab Company, which had a monopoly on the taxi concession in Cleveland for more than 50 years. When Browns players were moved off the active roster, they continued to be paid through the taxi company until they were active players again—hence, the "taxi squad."

Undefeated

In the history of the NFL, only one team has gone undefeated. The 1972 Miami Dolphins went 17–0 and won the Super Bowl that year. Two other teams, the New England Patriots in 2007 and the Chicago Bears in 1934 and 1942, went undefeated during the regular season and lost in the championship game.

But one other team in professional football went undefeated. The 1948 Cleveland Browns went 14–0, blowing through the AAFC. Buffalo beat Baltimore in an Eastern Division playoff game for the right to face the Browns in the AAFC Championship. It was like drawing straws for a firing squad. The Browns waxed the Bills 49–7 to finish the season 15–0.

The NFL recognizes the records of the American Football League of the 1960s because that league in its entirety became part of the NFL, but the AAFC is not recognized because only three teams from the circuit—the Browns, the San Francisco 49ers and the Baltimore Colts—joined the NFL when the AAFC folded after the 1949 season.

In all, the Browns reeled off 29 straight wins from 1947 to 1949.

Moving to the NFL

NFL commissioner Elmer Layden was scornful of the AAFC when it was founded, saying, "Let them get a ball, draw a schedule and play a game. Then I will talk to them."

Although the AAFC outdrew the NFL, averaging 38,310 fans per AAFC game to 27,602 fans per NFL game, it was limping along financially. Franchises were merging or folding, unable to stay afloat. The Browns were victims of their own success in the AAFC. Fans were used to them dominating the league and stopped coming out to see the games.

When the AAFC folded, the NFL took the Browns, the 49ers and the Colts. Both the Browns and the 49ers were competitive teams, but the Colts were brought along at the insistence of Washington Redskins owner George Preston Marshall, who saw the Baltimore-Washington rivalry as a boon. The rest of the AAFC players were spread among the NFL.

As the 1950 season dawned, the Browns were taken lightly by the established NFL, even after they went undefeated in their exhibition schedule, including a 38–7 routing of Green Bay at the Glass Bowl in Toledo. They would open the season against the Philadelphia Eagles, the defending NFL champions. Coach Earle "Greasy" Neale was confident, announcing that he didn't even scout the team. "They are just a basketball team," he said. "All they can do is throw the ball."

The Browns won 31–10, but that wasn't enough for Coach Brown. When the two teams met again, the Browns prevailed 13–7. And that was without a single pass attempt.

The Browns acquitted themselves well throughout their first season in the NFL. Their only two losses during the regular season were to the New York Giants. They would meet the G-men again in the playoffs, prevailing 8–3 on a frozen field at Municipal Stadium.

The win set up a championship game against the Western Division winners: the Los Angeles Rams. A nail-biter ended with Lou "The Toe" Groza booting a game-winning field goal, giving the Browns a 30–28 win and an NFL Championship in their first year in the league.

Toppling the Terminal Tower

In 1960, the Browns went up for sale. Among the people interested in buying the team was a 36-year-old Brooklyn native who worked in television advertising: Art Modell.

Modell bought the team for $3,925,000 in 1961. For comparison, in 1953, Mickey McBride had sold the team to a syndicate of investors (including Homer Marshman, who founded the Cleveland Rams in the 1930s) for $600,000.

Modell was a promoter at heart, engineering football doubleheaders and volunteering the Browns for the first Monday Night Football game in 1970. He was determined to be a hands-on owner, a concept that coach Paul Brown was not used to. In fact, Brown's contract said he had the final word for player-personnel dealings.

A fight was brewing, and it culminated on January 7, 1963. Brown was summoned to Modell's office and fired as coach of the Browns. There were allegations that the game had passed him by, that he couldn't be an effective coach to the current breed of NFL player. Some players thought that Brown treated them like children, and that he had a college rah-rah mentality that they didn't care for.

But he was still regarded as one of the best coaches in the game, and his removal as coach stunned Cleveland. The city was then in the midst of a newspaper strike, but a special 36-page booklet, "Paul Brown: The Play He Didn't Call," was distributed. A total of 50,000 copies were snapped up in days. In the booklet, columnist Frank Gibbons said that Brown's firing was like toppling the Terminal Tower, then the tallest building in Cleveland.

Brown had six years left on his contract at $82,500 a year, and the joke in Cleveland was that the only people who were paid more to play golf were Arnold Palmer and Jack Nicklaus.

The Acting Career of Jim Brown
Jim Brown was the go-to running back for the Cleveland Browns from 1957 until his retirement

in 1965, when he was the record holder in both career (12,312 yards) and single season (1863 yards in 1963) rushing yards, rushing touchdowns (106) and total touchdowns (126). He made it a point not to be an easy man to catch on the field. "Make sure when anyone tackles you he remembers how much it hurts," he said.

Jim Brown was born in Georgia but grew up in New York. He received scholarship offers from 45 different colleges but went to Syracuse University, which did not offer him a scholarship. At Syracuse, he excelled not just in football, being named an All-American, but in lacrosse as well.

In 1957, the Browns were still looking for a quarterback to replace Otto Graham, who retired after leading the Browns to the 1955 NFL Championship. There was no shortage of quarterbacks available in the draft, including John Brodie and Len Dawson. Paul Hornung, the "Golden Boy" of Notre Dame, was also available. The Browns had the fifth pick, and Paul Brown watched Brodie and Hornung get snapped up by San Francisco and Green Bay, respectively. The Browns lost a coin flip to the Steelers, who drafted Dawson. He spent two years in Pittsburgh and then two years in Cleveland, all with little success, before latching on with the Kansas City Chiefs and adapting to the wide-open game of the American Football League.

So with the top quarterbacks taken, the Browns gave Jim Brown a $3000 bonus and a $12,000 salary—at the time, the most ever for a rookie on the team.

Brown's numbers might seem quaint when compared to running backs such as Emmitt Smith and LaDainian Tomlinson, but one stat must be taken into account: in his NFL career, Brown averaged 5.2 yards per carry, still a league record. By comparison, Walter Payton averaged 4.4 yards per carry, and Emmitt Smith, 4.2 yards per carry. Brown was one of the great running backs, and for that, most Clevelanders, as well as scholars of the NFL, remember him. But the rest of the United States, even the world, knows him more for his thespian activities.

Jim Brown's career as an actor began while he was still playing in the NFL, when he appeared in the 1964 film *Rio Conchos*, a low-budget western starring Stuart Whitman and Richard Boone. Brown played a soldier who allied himself with a small band of gun-toting good guys out to stop an ex-Confederate army officer bent on revenge. The film was a mediocre success, but it got Brown interested in acting.

In fact, acquiring the acting bug led to Brown's retirement from football. After the 1965 season, Brown went to Europe to film *The Dirty Dozen*. He was late to training camp in 1966, and Browns owner Art Modell threatened to fine Brown. In response, Brown wrote to Hal Lebovitz of the *Plain Dealer* to announce his retirement, leaving Browns fans and football fans in general to wonder what might have been.

The Browns failed to make the playoffs in 1966, and lost in the Playoff Bowl—a game for third place in the NFL—in 1967. They lost the NFL Championship games in 1968 and 1969. Would Jim Brown have led the Browns to another championship—and potentially a berth in a Super Bowl?

Brown has had more than 55 television and movie roles, including appearances in the 1987 Arnold Schwarzenegger movie *The Running Man* and as the ex-boxing champion turned hero in the 1996 movie *Mars Attacks*.

In 2002, the camera was turned on Jim Brown when famed director Spike Lee released *Jim Brown: All-American*, a retrospective on Brown's professional career and checkered personal life.

Bernie

In the early 1980s, a lot of boys in northeastern Ohio had posters of Brian Sipe in their bedrooms. Sipe was the quarterback for the Kardiac Kids, leading the Browns in the late 1970s and early 1980s to a variety of last-second victories—and in a 1981 playoff game against the Oakland Raiders, a heartbreaking loss known to fans everywhere as "Red Right 88." Sipe was the Associated Press's NFL MVP in 1980.

One of Sipe's biggest fans was Bernie Kosar, who grew up as a Browns fan and a quarterback.

As a senior at Boardman High School in 1981, he was named Associated Press Player of the Year. Kosar wanted to go to Ohio State or Pitt, both within a couple hours of Boardman, but his throwing mechanics scared off most coaches. He ended up going to Miami, where he led the Hurricanes to an NCAA title as a redshirt freshman.

The following year, Kosar set school records in yards and touchdowns in a season, and was fourth in Heisman Trophy voting. After the 1984 season, he announced that he was going to turn pro, and that he wanted to play for the Browns. The Browns moved heaven and earth to comply, and the NFL ultimately ruled that Kosar, who would graduate in the summer, would be eligible for the supplemental draft. The Browns traded four picks to the Buffalo Bills for the top pick in the supplemental draft and chose Kosar.

Five games into the 1985 season, Kosar was the starting quarterback after Gary Danielson was injured. The Browns went 8–8 but won the AFC Central Division, making the first of five straight playoff appearances. They lost to the Dolphins 24–21.

In each of the next two years, the Browns won the AFC Central Division and advanced to the conference championship game. And in each game, they were beaten by the Denver Broncos. The first game came to be known for "The Drive," when Broncos quarterback John Elway—who, in contrast to Kosar, demanded a trade *from* the team that drafted him, the Baltimore Colts—led his team

98 yards down the field at Municipal Stadium to score a touchdown and send the game into overtime. Rich Karlis, a native of Salem, not far from Kosar's hometown of Boardman, booted a 33-yard field goal to send the Broncos to the Super Bowl.

In January 1988, the Browns clawed back from a 21–3 deficit in the AFC Championship game at Mile High Stadium and tied the game at 31. The Broncos scored to take a 38–31 lead, and the Browns were driving the ball and appeared poised to tie the game again when running back Earnest Byner fumbled just short of the end zone, with 1:05 left in the game. The Browns scored a meaningless safety on Denver's ensuing possession and lost 38–33.

Kosar injured his elbow in the 1988 season opener and ended up missing seven games as the Browns went 10–6. They lost their playoff opener.

In 1989, Kosar put up decent numbers, throwing for 3533 yards as the Browns went 9–6–1 under first-year head coach Bud Carson. They advanced to the AFC Championship, where once again, they lost to the Broncos.

The Browns sank to 3–13 in 1990. Carson was gone midway through the season, and owner Art Modell hired Bill Belichick, an assistant with the New York Giants. Kosar threw for almost 3500 yards in 1991, but the Browns finished 6–10 that year. They were a game better in 1992.

The Browns started 5–2 in 1993, but Kosar wasn't getting along with Belichick. They argued over playcalling, and after a loss on November 7 to, yep, you guessed it, the Denver Broncos, Belichick cut Kosar loose, citing diminishing skills.

Kosar signed with the Dallas Cowboys and backed up Troy Aikman, earning a ring when the Cowboys beat the Bills in Super Bowl XXVIII. He then finished out his career as a backup to Dan Marino in Miami.

Kosar tried to become a partner in an ownership group bidding for the expansion Browns in 1999. He even made peace with Belichick, who later said that he mishandled the situation.

Bill Belichick

In 1991, the Browns were once again looking for a new head coach. Bud Carson had been fired, and Art Modell decided to give another assistant his first head coaching job. Bill Belichick had never played professional football, but he began his coaching career in 1975, breaking down film in Baltimore for Colts coach Ted Marchibroda.

Belichick served as an assistant on two Super Bowl champion New York Giants teams. He remains the last Browns coach to win a playoff game, beating his mentor Bill Parcells 20–13 in a wild card game at Municipal Stadium on New Year's Day, 1995—also the day the last NFL playoff game in Cleveland was played.

Art Modell had high praise for the coach when he hired him, saying Belichick would win more Super Bowls than Don Shula. As it turned out, Modell was right, but Belichick went on to win them with the New England Patriots.

Moving the Browns

In November 1995, there was actually a rare feeling in Cleveland: optimism. The Indians had just finished their first World Series trip since 1954, and fans had every reason to believe that they would be back. The Cavs had started their third season under coach Mike Fratello, and everyone hoped for improvement from the previous year's playoff season. The Browns were coming off a playoff season as a wild card team. And the Rock 'n' Roll Hall of Fame, a gem designed by I.M. Pei, had just opened in September, next to Municipal Stadium.

But Art Modell pulled the rug out from under everyone when he announced the unthinkable: the Browns were moving to Baltimore. If his firing of Paul Brown was like toppling the Terminal Tower, moving the Browns was like detonating an atomic bomb on East Ninth Street.

Municipal Stadium was owned and operated by the city until Modell proposed operating the stadium in 1973. The city, about a hair away from bankruptcy, agreed, and Modell started the Stadium Corporation. The team would pay $150,000 to the city for the first five years of the 25-year lease, and $200,000 annually afterward.

The Stadium Corporation, 80 percent of which was owned by Modell, would keep all parking, concession and advertising revenue, and charge rent to the Indians.

Over the next few years, Modell found himself pouring money into the stadium to install luxury boxes and other improvements—while taking money from Stadium Corporation. Modell bought a plot of land in Strongsville for $800,000. He then sold the land to Stadium Corporation for $4 million, necessitating a $3 million loan to Stadium Corporation from the bank. That amount was paid to Modell in cash, with the rest in the form of a promissory note.

Meanwhile, Modell was telling the Indians that he needed to charge them more rent, and at the same time he was trying to unload the Stadium Corporation on the Browns for $6 million. Modell said that the corporation would be worth more if it was owned by the team instead of Modell. Robert Gries, who owned part of the Browns, voted against the sale, and when he was outvoted, went to court in 1986 to block the sale—successfully. So Modell was saddled with the stadium, at least through 1999.

Modell turned down an offer to be part of the Gateway Project, which in the early 1990s was building a new stadium where downtown met the highways that crisscrossed Ohio. Gateway turned into new homes for the Cavaliers and for the Indians, who were the largest single tenant for

Municipal Stadium. But Tribe owners had felt shut out at Municipal Stadium, since Modell didn't share revenues for luxury boxes, and it was more than a rumor that if they didn't get a new stadium, the Indians might move.

But it was the Browns that ended up moving. Modell said he had no choice but to move to Baltimore. He was losing money as owner of the Browns—a team that drew 70,000 fans per game, on average. In fact, in 1994, the year before the move, the Browns drew the highest local ratings of any NFL team.

Fans were outraged. Advertisers pulled their ads from the stadium. Modell, whose antics had irritated Browns fans for years, became public enemy number one.

Modell was given a sweetheart deal with a new stadium (including the sale of personal seat licenses), money for a new training facility and other expenses. But he was still stuck with a lease through 1999 at Municipal Stadium. And the day after the move was announced, Cuyahoga County voters resoundingly approved the extension of the "sin tax," which was used to build Jacobs Field and Gund Arena, and now would be used to finance renovations to Municipal Stadium.

The NFL stepped in and made an unprecedented deal. The Browns franchise would be regarded as inactive until a new expansion franchise was granted in 1999—contingent on the construction of a new stadium. The new franchise would retain the records, colors and history of the Browns. The franchise Art Modell owned would become known as the Ravens and be regarded as a new franchise. While the Colts took their history with them from Baltimore to Indianapolis, the Ravens would start from scratch.

The Browns were 4–4 when rumors of the move started to leak out. The season went downhill from there, as the Browns won just one more game, on December 17, 1995. It was the last game at Municipal Stadium, and it was against the Bengals—a team that was also approached by Baltimore officials before they made Modell an offer he couldn't refuse.

And the final, cruel irony? When Art Modell held the Vince Lombardi Trophy after the Ravens won the Super Bowl in 2001, his days as Ravens owner were limited. In 1999, Modell was still $185 million in debt, and in 2003, he agreed to sell all but one percent of the team to Steve Bisciotti. Modell, who once said that the key to making a small fortune in the NFL was to start with a large one, saw the value of his team increase exponentially in 40 years from less than $4 million to $600 million, the sale price to Bisciotti.

Modell had a football team in Cleveland, and then one in Baltimore. Either one of them should have been a license to print money. But he had to move the team, and then—after ripping the heart out of northern Ohio—sell it.

Cleveland Browns Head Coaches

Paul Brown	1946–1962
Blanton Collier	1963–1970
Nick Skorich	1971–1974
Forrest Gregg	1975–1977
Dick Modzelewski	1977 (interim)
Sam Rutigliano	1978–1984
Marty Schottenheimer	1984–1988
Bud Carson	1989–1990
Jim Shofner	1990 (interim)
Bill Belichick	1991–1995
Chris Palmer	1999–2000
Butch Davis	2001–2004
Terry Robiskie	2004 (interim)
Romeo Crennel	2005–2008
Eric Mangini	2009–2010
Pat Shurmur	2011–

The Birth of the Bengals

After Paul Brown was forced out of Cleveland following the 1962 season by owner Art Modell, the man who had spent the better part of 30 years as a football coach was suddenly idle.

He had no shortage of opportunities. John Galbreath, then the owner of the Pittsburgh Pirates, asked Brown if he was interested in becoming Major League Baseball commissioner. Brown, who had been suggested as a candidate for NFL commissioner in 1960 before owners ultimately decided on Pete Rozelle, declined. Brown's name was also suggested as part of a potential ownership group for the Philadelphia Eagles. When the Eagles were sold, he was then rumored to be a candidate for the head coaching job that went to Nick Skorich—who would later coach the Browns.

What Brown really wanted was to run the show for another pro football team—in Ohio. He set his sights on Cincinnati, a town that had had an NFL football team, the Reds, in 1933 and 1934, and teams representing various other leagues. But the Queen City had been without a pro football team since 1942.

The NFL was getting ready to expand in 1965, and Brown, as well as his son Mike, became officers in a corporation formed to bring football to Cincinnati. They established funding for a new multipurpose stadium on the bank of the Ohio River that would also be used by the Reds.

In 1966, it was announced that the NFL and the AFL would merge for the 1970 season. The merger had to be approved by Congress, and U.S. Senator Russell Long and U.S. Representative Hale Boggs—both of Louisiana—wanted assurances that the NFL would find a home in New Orleans. Rozelle agreed, the legislation passed, and the next NFL team was the New Orleans Saints.

But in 1967, the AFL came to town. They were looking to expand, and Brown found himself as the head of one of the syndicates vying for the new franchise. Another was headed by John "Socko" Wiethe, a prominent lawyer and former football player for Xavier University and the Detroit Lions.

Wiethe's team would be the Romans, and he had a deal with legendary college football coach Bear Bryant to become the first coach of the team.

Eventually, though, the AFL accepted Brown's pitch, and he was awarded the new franchise. A newspaper poll suggested naming the team the Buckeyes, and Wiethe's suggestion of the Romans was also pitched. But the team would be called the Bengals—no doubt partly in homage to Brown's alma mater. In fact, they wore black and orange uniforms, just like Massillon.

In 1970, the merger came through, and the Bengals were in the Central Division of the American Football Conference. Riverfront Stadium opened, and the Bengals won the first AFC Central crown, going 8–6. They lost to eventual Super Bowl champion Baltimore in the playoffs. They won another division title in 1973 and made the playoffs as a wild card team in 1975, Brown's final season as coach.

He stepped aside for assistant Bill "Tiger" Johnson, and finished his career with a record of 222–112–9, an astonishing .660 winning percentage. Brown remained with the team as president until his death in 1991. Today, not only is the stadium in Massillon named for him, but the Bengals also play their home games in Paul Brown Stadium.

The Freezer Bowl

On January 2, 1982, the San Diego Chargers prevailed in a 41–38 overtime game over the Miami

Dolphins at the Orange Bowl. *Sports Illustrated* called it "The Game No One Should Have Lost," and the image of Chargers tight end Kellen Winslow being carried off the field after the win has become one of the most iconic images in sports. Both teams sweltered through the game that was played in a humid 80°F.

And for their trouble, the Chargers got to face the Bengals at Riverfront Stadium the next week in the AFC Championship game, what is still the coldest NFL game ever played. The Bengals had beaten the Bills the week before for their first playoff win in team history.

The day of the game, newscasters were warning people to keep their pets inside. Water pipes and toilets froze at Riverfront Stadium. The temperature was –9°F, and with winds blowing between 25 and 30 miles per hour, the wind chill got down to –59°F. In a bit of gamesmanship, the Bengals linemen took to the field in short sleeves. They got out to an early lead and kept widening it, winning 27–17, thanks in no small part to four Chargers turnovers. The Bengals were going to make their first appearance in the Super Bowl.

They faced another team making its first trip to the Super Bowl, the San Francisco 49ers, coached by Brown's former assistant, Bill Walsh. The 49ers, led by quarterback Joe Montana, got out to a 20–0 halftime lead, and although the Bengals closed the gap, they couldn't win the game and lost 26–21. However, they were the first team to

lose a Super Bowl and outgain their opponent in
yardage, 356–275.

Cincinnati Bengals Head Coaches

Paul Brown	1968–1975
Bill "Tiger" Johnson	1976–1978
Homer Rice	1978–1979
Forrest Gregg	1980–1983
Sam Wyche	1984–1991
Dave Shula	1992–1996
Bruce Coslet	1996–2000
Dick LeBeau	2000–2002
Marvin Lewis	2003–

The Duke

Shortly after the end of the second game on the
night that the NFL's conference championship games
are played, workers at the Wilson football factory in
Ada—home to Ohio Northern University—start
making the balls for the Super Bowl.

More than 120 people work at the plant, which
was built in 1955. They turn out more than 700,000
footballs a year, including all the footballs for the
NFL (the Duke football, named for the late New
York Giants owner Wellington "Duke" Mara), the
NCAA, 27 high school football associations and
countless other leagues.

The factory produces 216 footballs the night of
the conference games—waiting until the games are
over to include the name of both teams on the
Super Bowl footballs—and ships them out to
each Super Bowl team Monday morning. Of each

team's allotment, half of the footballs are used for practice and the other half are set aside for the game.

Odd Position

Ohio native Ben Roethlisberger has done it all in his career as quarterback for the Pittsburgh Steelers. Since joining the NFL in 2004, he has been named the NFL Offensive Rookie of the Year, was selected to the Pro Bowl in 2007, and led his team to two Super Bowl wins and another Super Bowl appearance. Roethlisberger was born in Lima, but his family moved to Findlay. From the moment he first took to sports at Findlay High School, he showed himself to be a versatile athlete and an adept leader, being named captain of the football, basketball and baseball teams.

Roethlisberger's first love was basketball, but before his senior year, he attended a summer football camp—in Pittsburgh, of all places—and started to gravitate toward the gridiron. Roethlisberger was a natural as a quarterback his senior year, but that was the only year he took snaps. Prior to that, he played wide receiver, catching passes from quarterback Ryan Hite, son of the coach, Cliff Hite. The elder Hite, retired from coaching and now a state senator, said, "My son throwing to Ben was a better combination."

Hite insisted this arrangement was not nepotism, but he did admit that it might have been a minor oversight. "I'm a nationally known knucklehead," he said.

However, by playing in one of the positions he would later rely on as a quarterback, Roethlisberger was given a chance to experience the game from a different point of view and see the field in a different way. Perhaps that experience now aids Roethlisberger when he steps out of the pocket, gazes down the field and instinctively knows where to throw the ball for the wide receivers. So maybe Hite helped Roethlisberger become the champion quarterback he is today.

In one final irony, Roethlisberger went on to Miami of Ohio and to the Steelers playing quarterback. Ryan Hite went on to rewrite the Denison University record book—as a wide receiver.

College Football

Ohio State Football: The House that Chic Built

Ohio State played its first football game at Recreation Park on November 1, 1890, getting waxed 64–0 by Wooster. Recreation Park, a field east of German Village in Columbus, also served as home for the Columbus Buckeyes and Solons, two teams in the American Association in the 1880s. A historical marker of a Giant Eagle commemorates the site. Within eight years, home games were played at Ohio Field on North High Street. Original seating capacity was around 5000, but after some improvements and additions, the total capacity was raised to 14,000.

In 1916, the Buckeyes went 7–0, capping off the season with a 23–3 routing of rival Northwestern, to win the Western Conference (forerunner to the Big Ten) title. That year, Charles "Chic" Harley became the first Ohio State player to be named to Walter Camp's All-American team. Harley was a Chicago native (hence his nickname) but went to East High School in Columbus. He was offered scholarships to play football for Notre Dame, the University of Michigan and the University of Chicago, but he went to Ohio State.

When the United States entered World War I in 1917, Harley sought a position with the U.S. Army Air Service. While he was waiting for his commission, he played football for Ohio State, leading them to another undefeated season and conference crown.

Harley entered the service in 1918 but didn't complete training before the signing of the armistice that ended the war. In 1919, he was court-martialed for being found asleep in his bunk after 7:30 AM and sentenced to three months in the guard house, but as a result of intervention by the U.S. Secretary of War, the governor of Ohio and Ohio State University administrators, Harley was out in time for the 1919 season. The Buckeyes got their first win against the University of Michigan that year, 13–3, but lost the season finale against Illinois—Harley's only loss playing for Ohio State—to deny them a Western Conference crown.

The Illinois game had a record-breaking crowd of 17,000. At the time, football was, with a few exceptions (like the University of Chicago, Notre Dame and Michigan), the domain of the East Coast. But Harley's exploits—his running was described by James Thurber as a combination of music and cannon fire—put Ohio State on the map.

As early as 1913, Ohio State administrators and board members pitched the idea of a new, bigger stadium. But the recent success of Harley and the Buckeyes made it more than just a pipe dream. In 1920, a capital campaign was started for the new stadium. Within a year, $1 million was raised and ground was broken on the banks of the Olentangy River. The double-decked concrete stadium would have a horseshoe shape.

On October 7, 1922, the 66,000-seat stadium opened against Ohio Wesleyan. Only 25,000 fans showed up, leading some people to fear that the stadium might become a white elephant. Two weeks later, those fears were put to rest when the Buckeyes played Michigan in front of an announced crowd of more than 71,000.

After various additions and renovations, the capacity of Ohio Stadium is more than 102,000. The largest single renovation and addition came in 1999–2000, making the stadium's nickname, the "Horseshoe," a little disingenuous, as seats were added in the open end zone, effectively closing it. Since 1949, Ohio State has never been lower than fourth in the nation in attendance.

Woody Hayes

In 1950, after four years, Buckeyes head coach Wes Fesler was fired. Fesler's last game at Ohio State was a mortifying 9–3 loss to Michigan that is now known as the "Snow Bowl." Michigan had 27 rushing yards in the game, and Ohio State had 16. The Wolverines won without completing a pass or even getting a first down. All of Michigan's scoring came on defensive plays, both blocked punts. The first was a safety when a blocked punt squirted the ball out of the end zone, and the touchdown came when Tony Momsen blocked a punt by Vic Janowicz and fell on it in the end zone.

Paul Brown, who had won four AAFC championships and one NFL championship as coach of the Browns, was interested in the coaching job, but he had burned enough bridges at Ohio State that he wasn't considered. Don Faurot, then the head coach at the University of Missouri, was offered the job, and he accepted it before changing his mind two days later. He was told that Ohio State, having gone through three coaches since Brown's departure in 1944, was becoming known as a graveyard for coaches. Faurot ended up coaching Mizzou for six more years, with only one winning season, going 22–36 before retiring.

Instead, the Buckeyes got Wayne Woodrow "Woody" Hayes, an Ohio native who played college football at Denison, then taught and coached in high school before the outbreak of World War II, when he enlisted in the U.S. Navy. After getting out of the service, Hayes became head coach at Denison. His team went on a 19-game winning streak, including two undefeated seasons, and Hayes ended up getting hired to succeed Sid Gillman as head coach at Miami. While he was the Redskins' coach, Hayes went 14–5 and led Miami to a Salad Bowl win in 1950.

Ohio State took a flyer on the Ohio boy, and within four years, Hayes led the Buckeyes to an undefeated season, a Rose Bowl win and a national championship—the first for Ohio State since Paul Brown coached them.

Hayes spent 28 seasons at the helm of Ohio State. His tenure ended after the Gator Bowl on December 28, 1978, when Hayes punched Clemson's Charlie Bauman after he intercepted an Art Schlichter pass with 1:59 left to play in what turned out to be a 17–15 Tigers win. Hayes then took a swing at Ken Fritz, an Ohio State player who tried to intervene in the fracas. Ohio State got flagged for Hayes' unsportsmanlike conduct, and then got flagged again when Hayes went out on the field to yell at officials. The next day, Hayes was fired.

At the time of his dismissal, his career record of 238–72–10 made him the fourth-winningest coach in college football history. He went 205–61–10 at Ohio State. He won three consensus national titles, in 1954, 1957 and 1968, and two split titles, in 1961 and 1970. The Buckeyes won 13 Big Ten titles and appeared in seven Rose Bowls, winning four.

Hayes had 58 All-American players and two Heisman Trophy winners (one, Archie Griffin, is the only two-time Heisman Trophy winner in history). And Hayes had scads of assistants go on to bigger and better things. When he was fired, he was succeeded by former assistant Earle Bruce. Other assistants included Lou Holtz, Bill Arnsparger and Ara Parseghian (at Miami).

But one former assistant returned to bedevil Hayes during Ohio State's 10-year war with the University of Michigan, which Hayes referred to as "that school up north": Bo Schembechler. Schembechler, a Barberton native, played for Hayes at Miami and later served as an assistant for him at Ohio State.

Prior to Hayes' arrival at Ohio State, Michigan had beaten its rivals seven straight times. In his first 18 years as Ohio State coach, Hayes went 12–6 against the Wolverines. Then in 1969, Schembechler was hired to be the Michigan football coach. For 10 years, Hayes and Schembechler matched wits, and they appeared to be fairly even. Michigan won five games, Ohio State won four, and there was one tie. Each team made five Rose Bowl appearances in that span. The two teams shared six Big Ten championships. Ohio State won two outright league crowns; Michigan won one outright title and shared one with Michigan State. Today, the rivalry between Ohio State and Michigan remains, but it isn't as intense as it was during the decade when

Hayes and Schembechler scowled at each other across the sidelines.

Hayes was one of the first to admit that he wasn't the brightest bulb on the tree. Rather, he attributed his success to sheer work ethic. "There are a lot of people out there smarter than me," he said. "But they can't outwork me."

Jim Who?

In 13 seasons in Columbus, from 1988 to 2000, John Cooper compiled a 111–43–4 record, a .700 winning percentage. But he had two flaws that proved fatal to his coaching career: he couldn't win bowl games, with a 3–8 record, and more appalling, he couldn't beat Michigan, going 2–10–1 against the team Woody Hayes had referred to as "that school up north." Most galling were three losses to Michigan that prevented Ohio State from playing for a national championship. So Cooper was fired.

Ohio State cast a wide net looking for a new coach, but as it turned out, they only had to look about 180 miles away to find Jim Tressel, the coach at Division I-AA Youngstown State. They hired him as their new head coach in 2001.

Tressel might not have been a big-time college coach when Ohio State came calling, but he had a great pedigree. His father, Lee Tressel, was an Ada native who was recruited by Paul Brown to play football at Ohio State, but World War II intervened. Lee Tressel left Ohio State and ended up at Baldwin-Wallace College in Berea because the school had a V-12 program, which allowed high school graduates to go to college and train to become officers in the U.S. Navy.

Lee Tressel became a high school coach at his alma mater of Ada, as well as at Mentor—where Jim was born in 1950—and at Massillon before being named the coach at Baldwin-Wallace in 1958. He coached the Yellow Jackets for 23 years, compiling a 155–52–6 record and winning a Division III national championship in 1978. The following year, Lee Tressel was diagnosed with cancer. He died in 1981.

All of Tressel's sons—Jim, Dick and Dave—went to Baldwin-Wallace and played football for their father. Dick became a head coach at Gibsonburg High School and spent some time as an assistant before being named head coach at Hamline University in 1978, a job he held until he became part of Jim's staff at Ohio State.

Jim Tressel served as a graduate assistant at Akron, and then served as an assistant at Miami of Ohio and Syracuse before returning to Ohio to join Earle Bruce's staff at Ohio State. In 1986, Youngstown State named Jim Tressel its head coach.

Within five years, he won a national championship with the Penguins, beating Marshall 25–17 in 1991 to become the first and, to date, only father-and-son coaching combination to win college football national championships. That year was the first of four straight Penguin appearances in the NCAA Division I-AA National Championship game. The Penguins lost a rematch to Marshall in 1992, and then beat the Thundering Herd again in 1993. In 1994, the Penguins beat Boise State for their third national championship in four years.

In 1995, Tressel made an appearance on the national college football radar, vying for the head coaching job at the University of Miami, vacated by Dennis Erickson. Tressel was under consideration for the job when he withdrew his name. The U of M ended up hiring Butch Davis, and Tressel stayed at Youngstown State.

The Penguins beat McNeese State in 1997 for another national title, but they lost the title game to Georgia Southern in 1999. All told, Tressel went 4–2 in national championship games, and the Penguins made 10 playoff appearances.

Being an Ohio boy and a former assistant at Ohio State, Tressel had an appreciation for the Michigan game that appeared to elude John Cooper. When Tressel was introduced at a Buckeyes basketball game, he said, "I can assure you that you will be proud of your young people in the classroom, in the community, and most especially in 310 days in Ann Arbor, Michigan, on the football field." And he lived up to that claim, coaching Ohio State to a 26–20 win over the Wolverines at the Big House.

On May 30, 2011, Tressel resigned as Ohio State coach, amid investigations into wrongdoing by

Buckeyes football players. Tressel knew about the wrongdoing but failed to report the players to the NCAA, drawing a suspension of five games from the school. He was scheduled to go before the NCAA for punishment from them as well.

As head coach, Tressel went 106–22 in 10 seasons (by comparison, his predecessor, John Cooper, won five more games in three more seasons). Tressel went an astonishing 9–1 against Ohio State's most hated rival, Michigan, becoming the first Buckeyes coach ever to win seven consecutive games against the Wolverines. Under Tressel's watch, the Buckeyes have won outright or shared seven Big Ten titles and played for three national championships, winning one. He also tied a record with eight BCS bowl appearances. Tressel's 106 wins are good for third all-time at Ohio State, and his .828 winning percentage is tops among any coach who was there longer than three years.

The Cradle of Coaches

Paul Brown was one of many alumni or former coaches at Miami University in Oxford who went on to distinguish themselves as football coaches. As a result, the college has called itself the "Cradle of Coaches."

Brown was a Miami graduate, as was Weeb Ewbank, who was one of Brown's assistants in Cleveland before going on to be the only coach to win a championship in the NFL (with the Baltimore Colts in 1958, in "The Greatest Game

Ever Played") and in the AFL (with the New York Jets, who beat the Colts—coached by Don Shula, another former player for Brown and an Ohio native). Miami graduates have also distinguished themselves on the college level, including Red Blaik, who served as an assistant for the Redskins before going on to a long and illustrious career as head coach for Dartmouth and West Point, leading Army to back-to-back national championships in 1944 and 1945.

Other coaches who either graduated from or began their coaching careers at Miami were Woody Hayes, who won three national championships coaching at Ohio State; Bo Schembechler, who was Hayes' assistant at Ohio State before going on to coach the University of Michigan, winning 13 Big Ten titles; Ara Parseghian, who played for Brown with the Browns and won a pair of national titles at Notre Dame; and Sid Gillman, who coached at the University of Cincinnati and had a successful career as a head coach in the NFL and the AFL.

Coaches of more recent vintage who hail from Miami are Randy Walker, who coached at his alma mater before going to Northwestern; Ron Zook, formerly of Florida and now the head coach at Illinois; and Terry Hoeppner, who coached at Indiana. And Jim Tressel, an Ohio man through and through, was an assistant at Miami.

But the entire state can boast of its natives and coaches who have gone on to bigger and better things. Nick Saban, who played football at Kent State, was head coach at the University of Toledo and was Bill Belichick's defensive coordinator for the Browns, on a staff that at one point also included Al Groh (formerly at Virginia and briefly the Jets' head coach) and Kirk Ferentz (now at Iowa). Urban Meyer came from Ashtabula and was a head coach at Bowling Green State University. Bob Stoops at Oklahoma and Bo Pelini at Nebraska were teammates at Cardinal Mooney High School in Youngstown. In fact, the Stoops patriarch, Ron, was an assistant coach at Mooney. Les Miles of Louisiana State University is from Elyria. Brady Hoke, who just left San Diego State for the University of Michigan, is a native of Kettering, near Dayton. Mark Dantonio went to Zanesville High School and served as an assistant for Tressel at Youngstown State and Ohio State, and as a head coach at Cincinnati before becoming the head coach at Michigan State.

NFL coaching legend Chuck Noll is from Ohio; Noll, a former Steelers coach, hails from Cleveland. Jon Gruden was born in Sandusky while his father was an assistant coach at Fremont Ross High School. The elder Gruden was a head coach at Galion High School and Heidelberg, and Jon Gruden went to Muskingum College and then the University of Dayton.

All told, the Buckeye State accounts for less than four percent of the U.S. population, but 15 percent of major-college coaches are from Ohio. Of the past 12 teams that played for an NCAA

Football Bowl Subdivision National Championship, 10 were coached by Ohio natives or people who had coached in Ohio.

Mount Union Football

Nestled between Canton and Youngstown is Alliance, a small town spanning parts of Mahoning and Stark counties. The town is home to the University of Mount Union, which has, in the past 25 years, put together the winningest program in college football.

Larry Kehres, a Diamond native, was a quarterback for the Purple Raiders before graduating in 1971. Afterward, he was a graduate assistant at Bowling Green State University and spent a year as the head coach at Johnstown Monroe High School before returning to Mount Union. There, he spent 11 years as an assistant before becoming head coach in 1986. The Purple Raiders were respectable while Kehres was an assistant, and they won three Ohio Athletic Conference (OAC) crowns in his first seven years as head coach.

But in 1993, everything came together for Mount Union, as it went undefeated and won the Amos Alonzo Stagg Bowl to claim an NCAA Division III championship. In the next two years, the Purple Raiders won the OAC but failed to advance to the Stagg Bowl. Then they won six out of the next seven Stagg Bowls. They added national crowns in 2005, 2006 and 2008 with wins in the Stagg Bowl over Wisconsin-Whitewater. The

Warhawks and the Purple Raiders have met in six straight national championships starting in 2005; Mount Union has won three and Wisconsin-Whitewater has won three.

Kehres' record, going into the 2011 season, is 303–23–3 in 25 years as head coach. His .925 winning percentage stands as the best ever in college football—in any division.

The Heisman Trophy

John Heisman was born in Cleveland in 1869. The Ohio Historical Society has a marker commemorating his birthplace at a house on Greenwich Road in Seville. Heisman grew up in Titusville, Pennsylvania, an oil boomtown in the late 1800s. He went to Brown University and got a degree in law, but his first job after college was coaching a new football team at Oberlin College, where the field house now bears his name. His collegiate coaching career also included stops at Buchtel College (now the University of Akron), Clemson, Auburn, Rice, Washington & Jefferson and his alma mater of Brown, but he is probably best known for coaching Georgia Tech, leading them to 33 straight wins.

Heisman retired from coaching football in 1927, and in 1930, he became the first athletic director for the Downtown Athletic Club (DAC) in New York City. He also helped found the Touchdown Club in New York City, and what went on to become the National Football Coaches Association.

Heisman and the Downtown Athletic Club started giving out an award in 1935 to the best college football player in the country. The inaugural recipient of the DAC Trophy was Jay Berwanger of the University of Chicago. The iconic trophy of a ball carrier was modeled on Ed Smith, a New York University football player, and sculpted by Frank Eliscu.

On October 3, 1936, Heisman died of pneumonia, and directors of the club voted to rename the trophy the Heisman Trophy. That year's recipient was Larry Kelley, a native of Conneaut who played high school football in Pennsylvania and was an end for Yale.

Ohio State University is tied with the University of Southern California (USC) for the most Heisman Trophies won, with seven. However, USC's most recent Heisman winner, Reggie Bush in 2005, forfeited the trophy in 2010 for violations of NCAA policies, so there is no 2005 Heisman Trophy winner.

The Buckeyes have another Heisman distinction in Archie Griffin. In 1974 and 1975, the Ohio State running back and Columbus native became the only two-time Heisman winner, so Ohio State has had a total of six players with the Heisman Trophy: Griffin, Les Horvath (1944), Vic Janowicz (1950), Howard "Hopalong" Cassady (1955), Eddie George (1995) and Troy Smith (2006). All but George and Horvath were born in Ohio. Horvath was born in Indiana but raised in Cleveland.

In addition to the Ohio natives who won the Heisman Trophy for the Buckeyes, many other Ohio natives won the trophy for other schools. Frank Sinkwich of Youngstown won the Heisman Trophy in 1942. He played for Georgia, but by the time he received the award, he was wearing a different kind of uniform: that of the U.S. Marine Corps. Sinkwich's 382 yards of total offense remain an Orange Bowl record.

Dick Kazmaier of Princeton won the 1951 Heisman Trophy—to date, the last Ivy League player to receive the award. Prior to that, he was a five-sport athlete at Maumee High School, earning an incredible 17 letters. He served in the U.S. Navy, and although he was drafted to play professional football, he declined and got his master's in business administration and went into business. In 2007, Kazmaier, the namesake of Maumee's football stadium, donated his Heisman Trophy to his high school alma mater. It's on display at Maumee High School.

Cincinnati native Roger Staubach was also a Heisman last. To date, the 1963 winner from the Naval Academy is the last recipient of the Heisman Trophy from a U.S. service academy. Staubach quarterbacked the Midshipmen to the Cotton Bowl as a junior in 1963, and by the time he graduated from the Naval Academy, he owned 28 school records. After serving in the Navy for four years, Staubach had a stellar career for the Dallas Cowboys.

He is an inductee of the college and pro football halls of fame.

Two Ohio natives won the Heisman Trophy at Michigan, and both had their role in breaking the hearts of Ohio State fans everywhere. Desmond Howard, the 1991 winner, graduated from St. Joseph High School in Cleveland (an all-boys school that merged with all-girls Villa Angela in 1990 to form Villa Angela–St. Joseph), which can also claim as an alumnus former Michigan and NFL quarterback Elvis Grbac. Howard was a dazzling high school player and was highly recruited before deciding to go to Ann Arbor. Howard's junior year at Michigan saw him score 23 touchdowns—19 receiving—and haul in 61 passes for 950 yards. He also distinguished himself as a special teams player, breaking off a 93-yard punt return for a touchdown against Ohio State that inspired TV announcer Keith Jackson to say, "Hellooooo, Heisman!" In the NFL, Howard became the only special teams player to win Super Bowl MVP, thanks to a 99-yard kickoff return for a touchdown in Super Bowl XXXI for the Packers' win against the Patriots.

If Charles Woodson isn't the best athlete to come out of Fremont Ross High School, he has to be in the top five. He won the Ohio Mr. Football Award after his senior season in 1994. He gained more than 2500 yards and accounted for 230 points—including 38 touchdowns—for the Little Giants. Like Howard, Woodson went on to Michigan, and like Howard, he had a key punt return in a big win against Ohio State. Woodson, a cornerback who saw action as a receiver and on special teams, was the Big Ten Freshman of the Year, Defensive Player of the Year as a sophomore and then in his junior year, became the first, and to date only, primarily defensive player to win the Heisman Trophy. Woodson went out for the NFL draft after his junior year and was the fourth overall pick by the Oakland Raiders. He was named the NFL Defensive Rookie of the Year in 1998. After eight years in Oakland, Woodson went to Green Bay. He was named the NFL Defensive Player of the Year in 2010 and got a Super Bowl ring with the Packers in 2011.

The Dawn of the Forward Pass

Every year, hundreds of college students descend on Sandusky, a small city on the shores of Lake Erie, to work at Cedar Point. The amusement park, annually recognized as one of the best—if not the best—in the country, grew from humble origins as a playground and some bathhouses for people who wanted to change before going swimming in Lake Erie. It's also the place where, in 1913, the forward pass was perfected—by two students working as lifeguards.

In 1905, the International Athletic Association of the United States (IAAUS) was formed at the request of President Theodore Roosevelt, who told university presidents to reform the game of football or face its abolition. The game, at the time, lent itself to multiple injuries and even some fatalities because of lack of organization and mass plays like the flying wedge, where all players on offense took off downfield to run interference for a ball carrier. Some formations even allowed for teammates to grab each other as they moved downfield, bunching themselves together to form a wall for opposing players.

One of the rules adopted by the IAAUS—which became the NCAA in 1910—was the use of a forward pass, where an offensive player could throw the ball downfield to another offensive player. The first forward pass was believed to be completed by Bradbury Robinson, a native of Bellevue, who played for St. Louis University and completed a 20-yard pass to Jack Schneider. Robinson also threw the first incomplete pass, earlier in the game, which was a turnover per the rules of the day.

The forward pass was used successfully at St. Louis University, but only sporadically among major college programs until a pair of lifeguards at Cedar Point spent their spare time throwing a football back and forth to each other in the summer of 1913.

The two lifeguards went back to the University of Notre Dame in the fall. One, Charles "Gus" Dorais, was the team's quarterback. The other was a Norwegian immigrant named Knute Rockne. The Irish traveled to New York to play the U.S. Military Academy, one of the college football powerhouses of the day. Notre Dame was 3–0, and Army was 4–0, for the game on All Saints Day, 1913.

Dorais completed 14 passes in 17 attempts for 243 yards and two touchdowns—a good passing record today, but unheard of at the time. The Irish won 35–13, in a victory that made Notre Dame football national news.

"The yellow leather egg was in the air half the time, with the Notre Dame team spread out in all directions over the field waiting for it," the next day's *New York Times* said. "The Army players were hopelessly confused and chagrined before Notre Dame's great playing."

A plaque now stands on the beach at Cedar Point, commemorating Rockne and Dorais.

The First Penalty Flag

Irma Beede of Youngstown was called the Betsy Ross of football. Just as Ross sewed the first flag for the United States, Irma Beede sewed the first penalty flag for football.

Beede's husband, Dwight "Dike" Beede, was the football coach for Youngstown College (now Youngstown State University). At the time, officials noted penalties by blowing a whistle or a horn. Sometimes, fans and even players and coaches were unaware that a penalty was called because they were unable to hear it over the crowd noise.

Dike Beede came up with the idea for a penalty flag, and his wife sewed it together with cloth from their daughter's Halloween costume and an old bedsheet.

It was red and white, with a sinker from Beede's tackle box to weight down one corner.

The flags were used by officials during Youngstown College's game against Oklahoma City on October 17, 1941, at Rayen Stadium, and referees on the crew began using them elsewhere. Other officials picked up the idea, and in 1948, penalty flags became the industry standard. Today, the penalty flags are yellow and are weighted down with sand.

One of the original flags is on display in Stambaugh Stadium, now the home field for the YSU Penguins. The field there is named for Dike Beede. Rayen Stadium, located at The Rayen School on the north side of Youngstown, also served as home field for the Rayen Tigers and the Ursuline High School Fighting Irish in addition to the Penguins. When Stambaugh Stadium was built in 1982, Rayen fell into disuse. It was used a few times in the 2000s before the high school that was its namesake closed. Plans are currently being made to use the field again as a high school stadium.

Ohio Football Facts

- The Browns' team colors of orange and seal brown were taken from Bowling Green State University, the Browns' first training camp site, from 1946 to 1951.

- The Bengals' first home was Nippert Stadium, which has served as the home field for the University of Cincinnati since 1902. The stadium is the fourth-oldest playing site and fifth-oldest stadium in college football.

- The Browns hosted the first-ever Monday Night Football game on September 21, 1970, beating the Jets 31–21. Oddly, the Jets lost both the first and the last Monday Night Football games on ABC by the same score, falling 31–21 to the Patriots on December 26, 2005. Since then, the game has been shown on ESPN.

- In 1972, the Ohio High School Athletic Association started a playoff to determine state championships. Currently the OHSAA football postseason is five games in each of six divisions determined by enrollment. At its inception, the playoffs were two games in three divisions. The first Ohio high school football playoff champions were Warren Western Reserve (coached by Joe Novak, who went on to have some success in the college ranks as the coach at Northern Illinois), who beat Cincinnati Princeton, 37–6, in Class AAA (big schools); Akron St. Vincent–St. Mary, who beat Columbus Bishop Watterson, 28–7, in Class AA; and Marion Pleasant, who beat Lorain Clearview, 20–14, in Class A. The title games were at the Rubber Bowl in Akron (Class AAA), Paul Brown Tiger Stadium in Massillon (Class AA) and Ohio Wesleyan in Delaware (Class A).

Ohio Football Quotes

"Go out and play this game like you're a little kid again. This game is what you love to do. There should be nothing pressured about doing your job. It's what you grew up doing and always wanted to do. Just go out and play like you're a little kid again."

–Bengals wide receiver
Chad "Ochocinco" Johnson

"We have an emotional hold on this city unlike any other team has on any other city in America."

–Art Modell, on the Browns, two years
before he announced the move to Baltimore

"I have a great legacy, tarnished somewhat by the move."

–Art Modell—which is kind of like saying,
"Other than that, Mrs. Lincoln, how was
the play?"

"Because I couldn't go for three!"

–Ohio State coach Woody Hayes, when
asked why he tried a two-point conversion
against Michigan in 1968. The Buckeyes
beat the Wolverines 50–14.

"Anything easy ain't worth a damn."

–Woody Hayes

"Culturally in Ohio, football is something almost everyone is involved in. It's something everyone in Ohio has an affinity for."

–Jim Tressel

Chapter 2

Baseball: From Cy Young to Pete Rose, and Beyond

The Cincinnati Reds

The Original Red Stockings

The origins of baseball can be traced back to England, where a stick-and-ball game resembling baseball was played starting in the 17th century. During the great migration to the New World, the English brought their games with them, and by the 1800s, something similar to baseball was being played in the United States. It wasn't until 1846 that the first recorded baseball game took place with a set of codified rules, and at that time, baseball was still a fringe sport played mainly for fun. But in 1869, the Cincinnati Red Stockings changed all that when they became the first fully professional team.

The Cincinnati Base Ball Club formed in 1866 and played in the National Association of Base Ball Players. They fielded very successful teams from 1866 to 1868 and had a loyal following in the city. During this period, they earned the nickname

"Red Stockings" because of the distinctive socks they wore with their uniforms. However, unable to find enough local players, the Red Stockings turned to players from the East, and by 1868, about half the team was from out of town and were receiving some sort of compensation. With the best players at their disposal playing a professional league schedule, it was decided in 1869 that the entire team would make the switch to fully professional, with 10 men on salary for eight months.

On May 4, 1869, the Cincinnati Red Stockings played the first professional game, a 45–9 win over the hapless Great Westerns of Cincinnati. That year, they played more than 70 games across Ohio and the eastern states. The Red Stockings won all 57 regulation games in the National Association of Base Ball Players for the perfect season, a feat unmatched in professional baseball. But by 1871, running the team proved to be too expensive. The team folded, and many of the players from out east left for a new club in Boston called the Red Stockings.

In 1969, Major League Baseball acknowledged that year as the 100th anniversary of professional baseball, and the Red Stockings as the first professional team. Because Cincinnati has always been recognized as the birthplace of professional baseball, the Reds have always opened the season at home. They played the first game of the major league season every year from 1876 until 1989, with two exceptions: in 1877 and 1966, the Reds' home opener was postponed because of rain, and they opened the season on the road. Then in 1990, because of the lockout, the Reds opened 1990 in Houston. Even now, the Reds always open at home, even if television contracts lead to other teams playing the first game.

Back-to-back No-hitters

A total of 26 pitchers have pitched multiple no-hit games. Nolan Ryan leads the way with seven. Sandy Koufax had four, and Bob Feller, Larry Corcoran and Cy Young each had three. The Reds' Johnny Vander Meer is one of 21 pitchers who threw two no-hitters, but he stands alone in baseball annals as the only pitcher to throw no-hitters in consecutive starts.

In 1938, Vander Meer, 23, was in his first full major league season. On June 11, pitching at home at Crosley Field, Vander Meer twirled a no-hitter against the Boston Bees, as the Braves were called at the time. Although Vander Meer gave up three walks, no batter got farther than first base. He also struck out three players. Ernie Lombardi hit a home run in the 3–0 Reds win.

Four days later, Vander Meer's turn in the rotation came again. He was pitching against the Brooklyn Dodgers in the first night game at Ebbets Field. In 1935, Crosley Field became the first ballpark to install lights for nighttime baseball, and other teams followed suit upon seeing the Reds' increase in attendance.

The lights came on a little before 8:30, but a special program was planned, and the first pitch wasn't thrown for another hour. With one out in the bottom of the ninth, Vander Meer walked the bases loaded. Manager Bill McKechnie came out to talk to his pitcher, and Dodgers fans started yelling, "Leave him in!" Ernie Koy grounded to third, and the Reds went for the play at home. Two away. Leo Durocher came up for the Bums, and he worked the count to 2-and-2 before he popped out to end the game and give Vander Meer his second straight no-hitter.

That year, Vander Meer went 15–10. His career record, which also included a year with the Cubs and one start—his final one—with the Indians, was 119–121. From 1941 to 1943, Vander Meer led the National League in strikeouts.

Lombardi's Headache

Hall of Fame catcher Ernie Lombardi's Cincinnati Reds were down three games to none to the New York Yankees in the 1939 World Series. With the score tied 4–4 in the 10th inning of game four, the Reds could not afford a single mistake. But in the top of the 10th, they had dug themselves into a little trouble. With two outs, the Yankees had Frank Crosetti on third, Charlie Keller on first and Joe DiMaggio at the plate. DiMaggio hit what looked to be a single into right field, scoring Crosetti, but when Reds outfielder Ival Goodman let the ball roll through his legs, Keller and DiMaggio kept running. As soon as Goodman retrieved the ball, he whipped it back to home plate to stop the speeding Keller from putting the Yankees ahead by two. The ball arrived in Lombardi's glove a split second before

Keller delivered a vicious check that sent the ball flying into the air. As Lombardi sat dazed and confused, Keller touched the base for a two-run lead.

Seeing that Lombardi had been knocked into another dimension, DiMaggio made a break for home plate. But instead of picking up the ball that lay right beside him, Lombardi continued to sit in front of home plate, staring into space as DiMaggio scored the third run of the inning. The Reds could not mount a comeback in the bottom half of the 10th and lost the game and the series. It probably took Ernie Lombardi a lot longer to realize that the game was over.

Super Patriot

When the Detroit Tigers met the Cincinnati Reds for an exhibition game before the start of the 1942 season, everyone at the game was looking for something to keep their minds off the problems facing the nation. The United States had just entered World War II and sought solace from the horrors of war in patriotic displays. Before the start of the game, the crowd waited for the playing of the national anthem, but the public address system was broken at the time, so the game had to start without "The Star-Spangled Banner."

The first up to bat was Jimmy Bloodworth of the Tigers. On the first blazing fastball he got, Bloodworth smacked a hard grounder toward Reds second baseman Lonny Frey. It would have been an easy grab had it not been for a slight technical malfunction.

The public address system suddenly came to life and began belting out "The Star-Spangled Banner"!

Ready to pounce on the ball, Frey heard the anthem begin to play. Abruptly, he stood at attention with hand to heart. Frey's patriotism was so great that he failed to notice the ball bounce straight into the outfield.

Peter Edward Rose

Born in the city where he would become a legend, Pete Rose was the type of small teenager that many coaches would just look past. While many other kids his age would have given up on their pursuit of sports, Pete Rose tried even harder, launching himself full throttle into football and baseball. Despite his stature, he started at running back in his freshman year at Western Hills High School. However, he lost his starting position in his sophomore year and gave up on football for his first love, baseball.

While still in high school, Rose joined a Class AA team in Lebanon in the Dayton Amateur League and played every position he could, studying every facet of the game. He proved to be an adept student of baseball. In his first year alone, he compiled an incredible batting average of .500. Even with eye-popping statistics, pro scouts kept passing him by because of his size.

But the hometown Reds decided to give Rose a try after some prodding from his uncle, who had taken it upon himself to promote Rose. In 1960, right out of high school, Rose got a $7000 signing bonus and the promise of more if he managed to impress while playing for the Reds affiliate farm team, the Geneva Redlegs of the New York–Penn League. Playing at second base, Rose only hit .277 and had a few bad games in the field, but because he played every game like it was game seven of the World Series, he quickly became a fan favorite and was voted most popular player at the end of the year.

For his efforts, he was promoted quickly through the Reds farm system. In time, his batting improved and his fielding became near perfect. By 1963, the Reds felt confident enough to call Rose to the majors and give him a chance during spring training. He impressed the managers and coaches enough during exhibition games that he was given a spot in the lineup, making his major league debut on April 8 of that year.

Charlie Hustle

Since he began playing sports, Pete Rose always put everything he had into each play. He would sprint on and off the field at the beginning and ending of every inning, and he ran the bases each time as if he was in a 100-meter dash. Once, during his first spring training with the Cincinnati Reds, he sprinted to first base after drawing a walk against the New York Yankees. Legendary Yankee pitcher Whitey Ford spotted the young Rose's enthusiasm and gave him the nickname of "Charlie Hustle." Although Ford gave Rose the nickname derisively,

Rose adopted it as a badge of honor and throughout his career lived up to the name.

Rose Ruins a No-Hitter

On April 23, 1964, Houston Colt .45s pitcher Ken Johnson took to the mound against the Cincinnati Reds and nearly had one of the greatest moments of his career. With an ERA hovering around 4.00, Johnson was not the greatest pitcher in the Colts lineup, but that day against the Reds, he was unhittable. The only problem was that Reds pitcher Joe Nuxhall was also throwing a great game, not allowing a single run either.

In order to break the deadlock, someone would have to step up and try something different. That player would be Pete Rose, who tried to bunt his way on base in the top of the ninth. Rose connected, and the ball rolled slowly in front of the plate. Johnson raced off the mound, determined not to let the speedy Rose ruin the most memorable moment in his career. In his zeal to throw the ball to first, he tossed the ball over the first baseman's head, allowing Rose to advance to second on the error. Rose then found his way to third base after a ground out. The next Reds batter hit what appeared to be a ground out, but shortstop Nellie Fox committed an error on the play, allowing Rose to score.

Nuxhall completed his five-hit shutout in the bottom of the ninth, and the Reds went on to win the game 1–0 without recording a single hit.

Johnson could hardly believe his luck. He threw a no-hitter and still managed to lose.

Rise of the Big Red Machine

Bob Howsam was a minor league baseball executive in his hometown of Denver. Howsam, a disciple of Branch Rickey, joined his mentor when they tried to get a third major league off the ground—the Continental League. The league went away when Major League Baseball decided to expand, but Howsam helped bring a football team to Denver, the Broncos of the AFL. He was hired as a special assistant in the St. Louis Cardinals' front office in 1962 and was soon promoted to general manager. In 1967, he left St. Louis to become the general manager of the Cincinnati Reds.

At the time, the Reds had seen better days. Their last World Series title had come in 1940, and their last pennant, in 1961, seemed light years away. In 1964, when Howsam's Cardinals overtook the Phillies to win the pennant, the Reds finished second, one game back. Manager Fred Hutchinson died that off-season, and the Reds traded off many of their best players, including Frank Robinson. He was called an old 30 and was shipped to Baltimore for three players who amounted to little in the Queen City. Robinson went on to win a Triple Crown and an MVP award, and he led Baltimore to a World Championship in 1966. Meanwhile, the Reds were putting out feelers to move the team.

In 1967, a group of local investors bought the Reds for $7 million and made a deal to keep them in Cincinnati. They would share a new multipurpose stadium with the city's newest pro football team, the Bengals of the AFL.

Howsam set to work assembling a team that would become one of the most fearsome ever in Major League Baseball. The nucleus was there. In addition to Pete Rose, the Reds had signed a Cuban baseball player named Atanasio Perez, known to everyone as Tony. The Reds had also drafted a catcher from Binger, Oklahoma. Johnny Bench made his major league debut in 1967.

In 1969, the Reds made a run in the National League West in the first year the major leagues split off into divisions. But a West Coast swing took a beating on them, and they ended up finishing third in the West, which was won by Atlanta. The Reds fired Dave Bristol as manager and hired a minor-league manager with prematurely white hair: George Anderson, nicknamed "Sparky" because of his volatility.

Sparky Anderson was the third-base coach for the expansion San Diego Padres in 1969. He declined a coaching position for the California Angels after the season but took the job offer of managing the Reds. Fans and media in Cincinnati were justifiably skeptical. The *Cincinnati Enquirer* ran the headline, "Sparky Who?"

But whatever he did worked, as the 1970 Reds won the NL West with a record of 102–60. Earlier that summer, Riverfront Stadium opened and hosted the All-Star Game. The American League took a 4–1 lead into the bottom of the ninth in the Midsummer Classic, but the National League tied the game. Pete Rose struck out with two out to end the rally. In the bottom of the 12th, Rose came up to bat again. He singled off Clyde Wright (father of future Indians pitcher Jaret Wright) and advanced to second on a single by Billy Grabarkewitz. Jim Hickman hit a pitch into center field, and Rose wheeled around third and barreled toward home—and Indians catcher Ray Fosse.

Royals outfielder Amos Otis charged the ball and threw it in to the plate. Fosse wasn't going to get out of the way for the play, and Rose was running like he wasn't going to give way either. Rose hurled into Fosse, who never caught the ball. Rose was safe, and the National League won. Fosse separated his shoulder, and never lived up to his potential after that.

The Reds swept the Pirates in the National League Championship Series (NLCS) and faced the Orioles in the World Series. It was the first World Series played on artificial turf—in Riverfront Stadium—and the last played entirely in the afternoon. The Orioles won in five games, and Brooks Robinson was named MVP.

The Reds were still missing a couple of pieces. Injuries took a toll in 1971, and Cincinnati slipped to a tie for fourth in the division, with a record of 79–83. That season, the Reds traded for George Foster, who blossomed into a slugging outfielder and would be the only major league player to hit more than 50 home runs in a season between 1965 and 1990.

But the big deal came after the 1971 season, when slugging first baseman Lee May was dealt, along with Tommy Helms and Jimmy Stewart, to the Astros for Cesar Geronimo, Jack Billingham, Denis Menke, Ed Armbrister and a second baseman who'd been feuding with Astros manager Harry Walker: Joe Morgan. It was every bit as lopsided as the Frank Robinson deal, but this time in the Reds' favor. Morgan became a Hall of Fame second baseman, arguably the best ever at the position, and led the Big Red Machine to its glory.

In 1972, the Reds won the NL West by 10½ games, then beat the Pirates in the NLCS. This time, they would face the Oakland Athletics in the World Series. The A's were on their way to the first of three straight World Championships—the only team other than the Yankees ever to win three World Series in a row—but with their facial hair, colorful uniforms and even more colorful squabbling, they were regarded as little more than a sideshow act. The Reds took the A's to seven games before losing the series. Johnny Bench was named NL MVP.

The Reds won the NL West in 1973, but lost the NLCS to the Mets, who became the team with the worst record to advance to the World Series, going 82–79 and coming out of last place as late as

August to win the NL East. In 1974, the Reds finished second in the West to the Dodgers. Anderson was becoming legitimately worried that he'd be known as a manager who couldn't win the big one.

In 1975, Pete Rose was moved from the outfield to third base, allowing Foster to play regularly. The lineup was set now, and the Big Red Machine really started to roll. They won 108 games, the most by a team since the 1954 Indians won 111. They rolled over the Pirates in three games in the NLCS, and went on to face the Boston Red Sox—who had swept the Athletics in three games in the ALCS—in the World Series.

The Reds had a 3–2 series lead going into game six in Fenway Park, which turned out to be probably the greatest World Series game ever. The Red Sox jumped out to a 3–0 lead, but the Reds tagged Luis Tiant to tie the game up in the fifth. They went ahead 6–3 in the top of the eighth. With two on and two out in the bottom of the eighth, Sox manager Darrell Johnson called on pinch-hitter Bernie Carbo—a former Red. Anderson thought about lifting pitcher Rawly Eastwick, but left him in. He promptly gave up a three-run home run to Carbo, tying the game and leading Anderson to worry again that he would be known as a manager who couldn't close the deal.

The Red Sox ran themselves out of a rally in the bottom of the ninth, and the Reds couldn't score in the top of the 11th. Finally, in the bottom of the 12th, in the wee small hours of the morning, Carlton Fisk teed off on pitcher Pat Darcy and golfed a home run over George Foster and the Green Monster. The Red Sox won, 7–6.

Pete Rose promised Anderson that the Reds would win game seven and the series. But the Reds fell behind 3–0. With one on and one out in the top of the sixth, Tony Perez waited on a Bill Lee blooper and sent it over the wall in left-center field for a two-run shot. Rose singled home Ken Griffey Sr. in the seventh to tie the game. Joe Morgan hit a bloop single in the ninth to score Griffey again to give the Reds a 4–3 lead. It was the fourth game in which Morgan came up with a tying or go-ahead run on base in what turned out to be an MVP season for Morgan. Will McEnaney set down the side in the bottom of the ninth. The Reds were World Champions.

The 1976 season was almost anticlimactic. The Big Red Machine won the NL West in a walk, 10 games over the Dodgers, and this time rolled over Philadelphia in the NL Championship Series. They swept the Yankees in the World Series. Once again, they were World Champions, and once again, Joe Morgan was league MVP.

In 1977, George Foster was NL MVP when he hit 52 home runs, with 149 runs batted in. The Mets traded Tom Seaver to Cincinnati. But the Big Red Machine was being dismantled. Tony Perez was traded to Montreal, and the Reds finished second in the West. Howsam, not a fan of the new free agency in baseball, tried to trade for Athletics pitcher Vida Blue, but the deal was blocked by Commissioner Bowie Kuhn, saying he was trying to protect competitive balance. Shortly after that, Howsam retired as general manager.

The Reds had four former MVPs in the starting lineup (Bench, Rose, Morgan and Foster) in 1978, but finished second in the NL West again. Pete Rose had put together a 44-game hitting streak that year, setting a National League record, but it turned out to be a last moment of glory for a dynasty. Rose, who also got his 3000th career hit in 1978, signed with the Phillies in the off-season and went on to lead them to their first World Championship in 1980. And Sparky Anderson was fired.

The Reds won another division title in 1979 and had the best record in baseball in 1981; but in that strike-shortened season, the Reds never won in either half of the season and were left out of the playoffs. The Big Red Machine had sputtered out.

Are You Blind?!

Umpire Ken Burkhart made a mistake at the most important moment in his career in game one of the 1970 World Series between the Baltimore Orioles and the Cincinnati Reds. The Orioles were leading, 4–3, in the sixth inning, and Cincinnati was up at bat. The Reds had Bernie Carbo at third when Ty Cline hit a chopper directly in front of home plate. Orioles catcher Ellie Hendricks leapt up to field the ball while Burkhart focused on the third base line to see if the ball rolled foul, completely forgetting about Carbo, who was speeding toward home plate.

Not realizing that he was blocking Carbo's path to the plate, Burkhart was also directly in the way of Hendricks, who had fielded the ball and needed to get across to tag the runner. Simultaneously, all three men collided in front of home plate. Hendricks bowled over Burkhart to get at Carbo, but the wily runner slid past on the outside. The only person who could make the call was Burkhart, who ended up with his back to the play. Still, Burkhart was confident enough to call Carbo out.

The instant replay, however, showed that Hendricks had tagged Carbo with an empty glove while holding the ball in his bare hand. The replay also showed that Carbo slid wide, missing the plate completely; he only touched it by accident when he got up to argue the call. It would have been a difficult call to make even under the best circumstances, and Burkhart stuck with his original call.

It was the second time Burkhart had made a call like that against the Reds that year. Burkhart called Lee May out in a game July 12 against the Braves, but catcher Hal King had tagged May with an empty glove. Reds manager Sparky Anderson got booted for arguing that call.

This time, however, it was a crucial moment in the game. The Reds lost by that one run, with a final score of 4–3. They would eventually lose the World Series to the Orioles.

Anderson was philosophical about the call after the game. "Bernie Carbo would have been out easy if Burkhart wasn't in the way," he said. "That's why he can't be blamed for anything."

Sneaky Rose

Pete Rose was well known for doing anything to win a game. Even though the National League had won six straight games and 14 of the past 15 Midsummer Classics, Rose, ever the fierce competitor, was still looking for that extra edge over his opponents in the 1978 All-Star Game.

"There was all this talk going on about how the American League couldn't do anything against the National League," he said. "Well, I was always looking for ways to take advantage of that, kind of get under their skin and remind them in subtle ways that they really weren't as good as us."

Rose chose psychological warfare as his tactic. He came up with a scheme to make his National League hitters look a lot more powerful than they actually were. He ordered dozens of baseballs from the Japanese sporting goods company Mizuno. Their balls were made smaller and sewn tighter, which meant they carried much farther than major league baseballs did. Rose managed to sneak the balls into the stadium prior to the big game just in time for batting practice. After getting his National League teammates on board, Rose sent the balls out on the field for batting practice. Under false pretenses, Rose went into the American League clubhouse and convinced many of the players to come out and watch the practice.

"Everyone was hitting them out of the park," recalled Larry Bowa, second baseman for the Philadelphia Phillies. "It made me feel like Babe Ruth blasting those babies out of there."

After their practice was over, they quickly gathered up all the Japanese balls and sat down to watch the American League batting practice.

"We thought it was funnier than hell," continued Bowa. "We sat around and watched the American League take their batting practice. They were just barely hitting them to the outfield wall. It was normal stuff, but after the way our balls were flying way up high into the stands, the American Leaguers looked like little leaguers."

Whether or not it was that the American League was distraught after seeing the National League's batting practice that made them lose the game cannot be known, but Pete Rose will always swear by it. The National League won their seventh straight All-Star Game by a final score of 7–3.

"A Sad End to a Sorry Episode"

Pete Rose helped the Phillies win their first World Series in 1980. He was released by the team in 1983, and after a brief sojourn to Montreal—where he got his 4000th hit—he returned to the Queen City in 1984, where he was named player/manager. The old vestiges of the Big Red Machine were gone. Joe Morgan was finishing out his career in his hometown of Oakland. Johnny Bench had retired. George Foster was a Met. Only Davey Concepcion remained.

As manager of the Reds, Rose got his 4192nd hit on September 11, 1985, against the Padres at Riverfront Stadium, breaking the record held by Ty Cobb for most hits in a career. Rose retired as a player after the 1986 season, but he remained the Reds' manager.

In 1988, Rose ran afoul of National League president A. Bartlett Giamatti. Rose got into a shouting match with umpire Dave Pallone and bumped him, violating baseball's code of conduct. Giamatti suspended Rose for 30 days.

The following year, Giamatti was anointed as Peter Ueberroth's successor as baseball commissioner. Rose met with Ueberroth and Giamatti in February about allegations that he bet on baseball, and more specifically that he bet on the Reds. There is a rule in major league clubhouses from San Diego to Boston and all points in between: no betting on baseball.

Rose denied everything, but Major League Baseball retained Washington attorney John Dowd to investigate the matter more fully. Dowd's findings, though they did not reveal a "smoking gun," were damning. There were no tapes of him placing bets. But bookies and intermediaries told Dowd that Rose bet on baseball.

Rose, in turn, accused Giamatti of passing judgment on him before the facts were in and filed suit against Giamatti, Major League Baseball and the Reds. A Cincinnati judge issued a restraining order,

saying that Rose couldn't be fired as Reds manager
and that MLB couldn't act against him.

On August 24, 1989, Giamatti dropped a bomb-
shell at a news conference in New York City. Major
League Baseball had worked out a deal with Rose:
he would drop his lawsuit, and in turn, he would be
banned from baseball. The agreement specified that
Rose admitted nothing about whether or not he bet
on baseball. However, in his 2004 autobiography,
Rose admitted betting on baseball and on the Reds.

Giamatti called the ban "a sad end to a sorry episode." He said, "This whole episode is about whether
you live by rules or not."

Nine days after the ban, Giamatti died of a heart
attack. Fay Vincent was named commissioner, and
after two years, was forced out by the owners.
Brewers owner Bud Selig has been commissioner
ever since. Rose applied to both Vincent and Selig
for reinstatement, unsuccessfully.

In 1990, Rose was convicted of income tax eva-
sion and was sentenced to five months in prison.
But he remains in baseball limbo. An exception
was made for him to appear on the field in 1999
when he was named to baseball's All-Century
team. He has never—and because of his ban, will
never—come up for election to the Baseball Hall of
Fame. And although nobody other than his son
Pete Jr. has worn his uniform number 14 with the
Reds, the team has not retired it.

The Cleveland Indians

Hugh "One Arm" Daily

Although it is not known who might have been the first disabled player in professional baseball, a surprising number of athletes with various physical disadvantages have made it to the majors.

One of the first and most successful of these players was Hugh "One Arm" Daily, who pitched in the National League, Union Association and American Association from 1882 to 1887.

In 1883, Daily proved that he was one of the best players in the game. While pitching for the Cleveland Blues, he threw a no-hitter against Philadelphia, and just one year later, he led all Union Association pitchers in strikeouts. Lacking the use of his left arm, Daily was able to perform minor fielding duties by attaching a pad to his shoulder and blocking the ball should it come his way.

Really?

Just because someone asks does not mean you have to say yes! Cleveland Spiders manager Joe Quinn and his team were visiting Cincinnati to play the Reds for the final series of the 1899 season. Eddie Kolb, a 19-year-old cigar-stand clerk, happened to be working at the hotel where the Spiders were staying, and he kept asking manager Joe Quinn to let him pitch for Cleveland. After Kolb nagged the manager for several days, Quinn finally gave in and let Kolb pitch for Cleveland in the next game. The kid ended up pitching all nine innings, yielding 18 hits and five walks en route to a 19–3 loss—not the greatest move in baseball management history.

Cleveland Speaks

Never underestimate the power of the masses. Prior to the 1908 season, the major leagues had a rule that any game that was stopped was called a win for the team that led at the time of stoppage. But after the Indians lost the pennant to Detroit by the margin of one of these "half" games, Cleveland fans rose up and began a series of noisy protests at games and in front of league offices. So in 1909, the league bowed to the protesters and introduced a rule that said any called-off game having a mathematical bearing on the pennant race had to be made up.

Death by Pitch

On August 16, 1920, Cleveland Indians shortstop Ray Chapman became the only player in the history of Major League Baseball to die as a result of an injury on the field.

The Indians were in the middle of a pennant race and had come to New York to take on the Yankees at the Polo Grounds on a dark, wet, dreary afternoon. Pitching for the Yankees was Carl Mays, who was one of the players dealt by the Red Sox to New York during a fire sale. He was a sidearm pitcher, described as having a pitching motion that looked almost like he was throwing underhanded. He threw a pitch to Chapman, who probably didn't see the ball; he made no effort to move out of the way and was struck in the temple. The ball bounced back to the pitcher's mound, and Mays, thinking that Chapman had hit the ball, threw to first base.

Chapman was knocked unconscious, but he was revived and left the field under his own power. But when he got to the dugout, he collapsed again. Indians player/manager Tris Speaker was optimistic about his shortstop's condition, but Chapman died about 12 hours later from head trauma.

Speaker rallied his players around Chapman's death, and the Tribe went on to win the American League pennant, thanks to contributions from Chapman's replacement at shortstop, future Hall of Famer Joe Sewell. The Indians then beat the Brooklyn Dodgers, five games to two, in the last World Series played in the best-of-nine format. Indians players voted Chapman's widow a full winner's share from the World Series.

Mays continued to pitch until 1929, despite calls for him to be banned from baseball as a headhunter. He then served as a scout for several teams—including the Indians—before dying in 1971.

A plaque memorializing Ray Chapman was hung in League Park shortly after his death. When the Indians moved to Municipal Stadium, the plaque was moved there as well, but it was lost in the move to Jacobs Field in 1994. The plaque was found in storage and, after being restored, is now in Heritage Park, beyond center field at what is now called Progressive Field.

One in a Million

To throw a perfect game, a pitcher must retire 27 batters without allowing a single opposing player on base. In the history of Major League Baseball, a total of 20 perfect games have been thrown. It is known as one of the most difficult accomplishments in the sport. But, amazingly, there is another play that happens even less often.

The unassisted triple play, when a player on defense makes three outs by himself in one continuous sequence, remains one of the rarest moments in baseball because it relies on the proper confluence of factors and sheer luck. There must be no outs in the inning, and there must be at least two runners on base. In addition, the two runners on base have to run on a pitch, as in a hit and run, and the batter must then hit the ball to an infielder. The unassisted triple play has been successfully completed only 13 times in major league history, and only once during the World Series, in 1920 by Indians second baseman Bill Wambsganss.

In the fifth inning of game five, the Brooklyn Dodgers had no outs. Two runners were on first and second base when Clarence Mitchell stepped up to bat. Mitchell sent a line drive toward Wambsganss, known as Wamby to his teammates. At the crack of the bat, the two Brooklyn players took off expecting the ball to go into the outfield, but Wambsganss speared the ball out of the air to retire the batter. He then tagged second to get the lead runner. Then he tagged out the runner sprinting to second base.

Clarence Mitchell came up again in the eighth inning with a runner on first. He grounded into a double play and ended up accounting for five outs in two at-bats. Cleveland won the game by a score of 8–1 and the series by five games to two.

That same game is famous for another rare moment in baseball history: Cleveland Indian Elmer Smith hit the first ever grand slam in the World Series. With the Indians' triple play and grand slam, the Brooklyn Dodgers had no chance of winning.

Neal Ball of the Cleveland Naps was the first player in the modern era of baseball to record an unassisted triple play in a game on July 19, 1909, against the Boston Red Sox. In fact, until 1994, every unassisted triple play recorded in baseball involved a Cleveland player. In addition to Ball and Wamby's triple plays, three Cleveland players hit into unassisted triple plays: Frank Brower on September 14, 1923; Homer Summa on May 31, 1927; and Joe Azcue on July 29, 1968. The first unassisted triple play that didn't involve the Indians was when John Valentin of the Red Sox turned three against the Twins on July 15, 1994.

Mom!

What better way to honor your mother than to have her sit in VIP seats while she watches her son pitch a game in the major leagues on Mother's Day? That's exactly what Cleveland Indians pitcher Bob

Feller did on Mother's Day, 1939, but things did not turn out as he planned.

"I went the full nine innings that day, but Mom didn't," Feller later said.

Feller's parents sat in the front row seats along the first base line for the game against the Chicago White Sox. In the third inning, Feller was giving another ace performance, to the delight of his very proud mother. But then Marv Owen stepped up to the plate, and the happy Mother's Day mood changed very quickly.

Feller whipped one of his infamous fastballs at Owen, who managed to get a piece of it, fouling a hard line drive into the stands along first base. It headed directly for the crowd. Everyone in the stands managed to get out of the way except for Feller's mother. The ball smacked her in the head with such force that it broke her glasses and put a cut on her face that needed eight stitches to close.

Feller immediately ran from the mound to check on her. Like a true mother, she didn't want to ruin her son's big moment. So, she looked at her son with a face full of blood and told him that she would be all right. She ended up spending two weeks in the hospital.

Feller struck Owen out and went on to complete a 9–4 victory over the White Sox. He dedicated the victory to his mom.

The following year, Feller got tickets for his parents for another game against the White Sox in

Comiskey Park. This time, his mother got to see (albeit on a cold day) Feller throw a no-hitter, which remains the only no-no ever thrown on Opening Day, and the only game where the players on a team had the same batting average after the game as they did before: .000!

More than 50 years later, Bob Feller was watching another Opening Day no-hitter, and he didn't like it. On April 4, 1994, the Indians opened Jacobs Field. Feller, along with President Bill Clinton and Ohio governor George Voinovich (a former Cleveland mayor), threw out a ceremonial first pitch. Feller then watched Randy Johnson of the Mariners throw seven no-hit innings against the Tribe. Tom Hamilton, the longtime radio voice of the Tribe, remembered Feller pacing around upstairs.

"I was concerned," Feller said.

But Sandy Alomar laced a single into right field for the Indians' first hit in the new ballpark. Johnson ended up leaving the game that inning, and got a no-decision. The Tribe got the 4–3 win in the 11th inning when Wayne Kirby singled home Eddie Murray.

Indians End the Streak!

The "Yankee Clipper," Joe DiMaggio, began a hitting streak with a measly single off Chicago White Sox pitcher Eddie Smith on May 15, 1941. Two months later, DiMaggio's streak had stretched to 56 games when he smashed a double and two singles against the Cleveland Indians at League Park on

July 16. DiMaggio had overtaken the modern major league record of 41 games by George Sisler, as well as Willie Keeler's ancient mark of 44 games.

At the time, the Indians alternated between League Park on the East Side of Cleveland and Municipal Stadium. League Park, built in 1909, held a little more than 21,000 fans. The adjective most often used to describe Municipal Stadium, opened in 1932 on the shore of Lake Erie in downtown Cleveland, was cavernous. Correctly anticipating a huge crowd, officials held the next day's game at Municipal Stadium. It drew more than 67,000 fans.

In his first at-bat against starter Al Smith, DiMaggio laced a grounder down the third base line, but third baseman Ken Keltner reached over, backhanded the ball and threw Joltin' Joe out at first base. Smith walked DiMaggio in his second at-bat, and then DiMaggio came up in the seventh inning. Again he smacked a ball down the third base line, and again Keltner made the play, snaring the ball and throwing DiMaggio out at first. DiMaggio came up for the last time in the eighth inning, with one out and the bases loaded. The pitcher was now Jim Bagby, whose father of the same name was the first pitcher to hit a home run in the World Series, in 1920 for the Indians. Bagby got DiMaggio to ground out to Lou Boudreau at shortstop, who turned two.

It looked like DiMaggio might get a fifth at-bat in the game. In the bottom of the ninth, the Indians scored two runs. They were down 4–3 with the tying run on third and no outs. If the game went to extra innings, DiMaggio might come to the plate again. But the runner ended up getting caught in a rundown and was tagged out between third and home, and the Yankees went on to win 4–3. The streak was over.

During his streak, DiMaggio's batting average was .408, with 91 hits in 223 at-bats. It wasn't even the longest hitting streak of DiMaggio's career. While a rookie with the San Francisco Seals in the Pacific Coast League in 1933, he hit in 61 straight games, setting a league record. And after this hitting streak ended at Municipal Stadium, he went on another 16-game hitting streak. All told, he hit safely in 72 out of 73 games.

Joltin' Joe finished the season with a .357 batting average, a league-leading 125 RBI and 30 home runs. He was named American League MVP, the second of three times he would claim the honor.

Since the hitting streak, nobody has come within 10 games of matching it. The closest was Pete Rose, with a 44-game hitting streak in 1978.

The One You Don't Make

Many teams have found themselves on the short end of a trade. But sometimes, they hold off on the deal long enough to realize the potential error of their ways.

Indians shortstop Lou Boudreau became manager in 1942 at the age of 24. He was called the "Boy Manager." In 1946, a syndicate led by Bill Veeck bought the Indians. Veeck's father was an executive for the Cubs, and Veeck had owned the minor league Milwaukee Brewers. He liked to keep the team moving, prompting Boudreau to say later, "We always had three teams—one on the field, another coming and another one going."

Boudreau's contract was up in 1947, and Veeck shopped his shortstop around. A deal to trade him to the St. Louis Browns was so close that Veeck was ready to introduce Al Lopez as the new Tribe manager, but after fans and the press got wind of it, the tide of public opinion came in strongly against the deal. He gave Boudreau a two-year contract.

In 1948, everything came together. Boudreau batted .355 with 18 home runs and 106 RBI. The Indians were tied with the Red Sox and went to Fenway Park for a one-game playoff. In a move that mystified everyone, Boudreau chose rookie Gene Bearden as the starting pitcher for the playoff on only a day's rest, despite the fact that there were better, well-rested pitchers on the team. To top it off, Bearden was a lefty, facing a team with lots of right-handed hitters and a short left field wall. But apparently Boudreau knew what he was doing. He homered twice in the game, and the Indians won 8–3 to go on to the World Series for the first time since 1920. The Indians won the World Series against the Boston Braves in six games.

Boudreau was named the league's MVP. Although he was fired two years later, he remains the Indians manager with the most wins, and the last Indians manager to win a World Series, proving the old baseball saying that sometimes, the best trade is the one you don't make.

Satch's Rules to Keep Young

In 1948, the Indians signed ageless wonder Leroy "Satchel" Paige, who had a lengthy and illustrious career pitching in the Negro Leagues. Paige also barnstormed against major league All-Star teams. The signing was derided as another publicity stunt by Bill Veeck, but Paige went 6–1 down the stretch, and the Indians had to win a playoff game to win the pennant, so every victory counted.

Years later, Paige pitched for the St. Louis Browns in 1953—another team owned by Veeck—and in 1965, he threw three innings in a spring training game for the Kansas City Athletics. He always liked to keep an air of mystery about his age (telling a Congressional committee that his birth certificate was in the family Bible, but it was eaten by a goat, which lived to be 27 years old), but he was born on July 7, 1906, making him 42 when he played for the Indians, 47 when he pitched for the Browns and a young 58 when he pitched for the A's.

Paige had six rules for keeping young, and he used to keep them on a business card that he would pass out to people he met. The rules are:

• Avoid fried meats, which angry up the blood.

- If your stomach disputes you, lie down and pacify it with cool thoughts.

- Keep the juices flowing by jangling around gently as you move.

- Go very light on the vices, such as carrying on in society. The social ramble ain't restful.

- Avoid running at all times.

- Don't ever look back. Something might be gaining on you.

1954: A Season to Remember... and Then One to Forget

The Indians were headed back to the World Series in 1954. They had won 111 games, led by a pitching staff of Bob Lemon, Early Wynn, Mike Garcia, Art Houtteman and Bob Feller, who was getting older but still had a little left in the tank. Bobby Avila led the American League with a .341 batting average, and Larry Doby had 32 home runs and 126 RBI, both league-leading totals. The Indians would face off against the New York Giants, led by center fielder Willie Mays.

Game one at the Polo Grounds set the tone for the series. Vic Wertz hit a two-run triple to put the Indians on the board in the first inning. But he became better known for his at-bat in the eighth inning. Facing reliever Don Liddle with Doby on second and Al Rosen on first, Wertz launched a ball to center field. Mays broke to make the catch, losing his hat but pulling down the ball, at least 460 feet away from home plate. He wheeled around and threw it to the infield. Doby, who was running at the crack of the bat, had to return to second to tag up and only advanced to third. Rosen stayed at first. Liddle was pulled after facing Wertz, and as he came into the dugout, he said, "Well, I got my man."

In the bottom of the 10th, Dusty Rhodes came to the plate to pinch hit. Bob Lemon was pitching. Rhodes hit a ball to right field, 261 feet but over the fence. It was a three-run homer, and the Giants won 5–2.

In any ballpark but the Polo Grounds, Wertz would have hit the home run and Rhodes would have flied out. But the first game was a backbreaker for the Tribe, who went on to be swept by the Giants.

"They say anything can happen in a short series," Indians manager Al Lopez said. "I just didn't expect it to be *that* short."

The Giants moved to San Francisco in 1958 and wouldn't win a World Series for that city until 2010. The Indians wouldn't return to the World Series until 1995.

Sneaky Francona

The rules of baseball were meticulously formulated to create a free flowing, fair game that provides the best entertainment for fans. But as any player will tell you, rules are meant to be broken. In a game between the visiting Cleveland Indians and the

Boston Red Sox on June 11, 1962, Indians first base-man Tito Francona proved it.

In a dull, scoreless game, the Indians managed to load the bases late into the evening and stood poised to put away the game with one run. All Red Sox pitcher Earl Wilson needed was a ground out to finish off the inning. As Wilson went into his windup to deliver the next pitch, Francona, the runner on first, yelled out, "Hold it, Earl! Hold it!"

Thinking a time-out had been called, Wilson held onto the ball and stepped away from the mound. Unfortunately, a time-out had never been called, and because Wilson broke his pitching motion, the umpire had no choice but to call a balk. Wilson looked back at first base where he had heard the call for a time-out and saw Francona waltzing his way to second base with a huge smile on his face. The bases-loaded balk gave the Indians a 1–0 lead.

Red Sox manager Mike Higgins raced from the dugout and protested vehemently in the face of the umpire. Higgins quickly reminded the umpire of Section 4-06 of the official rules of Major League Baseball: "No player shall call time or employ any other word or phrase or commit any act while the ball is alive for the obvious purpose of trying to make the pitcher commit a balk." But luckily for Francona, none of the umpires had heard of the infraction and would not reverse the play.

Still stewing from Francona's trick, Wilson lost his concentration and fell apart in the inning. By the time he retired the side, Wilson had lost his shutout, giving up four runs.

Two innings later when Francona stepped up to the plate, Wilson was looking for revenge. He threw a fastball directly at Francona's mid-section, but the clever Indians first baseman got out of the way. Wilson was not yet done with Francona. On the next pitch, Francona hit a ground ball toward first, and as Wilson ran to cover first base, he just missed Francona with a vicious body check.

The Indians held on to win the game, and when later asked by reporters about the incidents, Francona just smiled and refused to comment. He knew he had gotten away with a suspect call and decided it was best this time not to say a word.

Bad Idea

Under the ownership of Bill Veeck in the 1940s, the Indians were known for some excellent promotions. Veeck largely invented the concept of people coming out to the ballpark for events other than baseball, be they a mock funeral for the pennant, like he did in Cleveland in 1949, sending a midget up to bat, like he did when he owned the St. Louis Browns (and he feared this event would be on his tombstone) or a scoreboard that shot off fireworks, like he had at Comiskey Park when he owned the White Sox.

However, the promotion on June 4, 1974, at Municipal Stadium went down in history—for all the wrong reasons. Stroh's Beer held a promotion for that night's Indians game against the Rangers: 10-cent beer night. The Indians at the time were owned by Ted Bonda, and the Rangers had recently had a successful 10-cent beer night.

So that June night, more than 25,000 people came to the Indians game, when the Tribe was averaging around 8000 per game. The crowd still looked small in Municipal Stadium, which at its peak held more than 90,000 fans. Those who did come just couldn't pass up 10 ounces of beer for 10 cents. Demand was so high that people stopped going to the concession stand and started getting their beer from Stroh's trucks behind the outfield.

Of all the teams that could have come to town for this bubbling mixture of alcohol and idiocy, the Rangers, managed by Billy Martin, who never met a fight he couldn't insert himself into, were probably the worst choice. In a recent game in Texas, the Indians were treated to some chin music, and a brawl ensued.

During this game, chaos reigned. A fan threw a firecracker into the Rangers' dugout. Streakers ran across the field. Rangers first baseman Mike Hargrove was almost conked on the head with a Thunderbird (the bottle of wine, not the car).

Then in the ninth inning, the Indians tied the game at five, and the potential winning run was at second base when a fan hopped down and took Rangers outfielder Jeff Burroughs' cap. Burroughs ran after the guy, who went back into the stands, but other fans stormed the field. So Martin, wielding a fungo bat, yelled, "Let's go get him, boys," and led his team out to Burroughs in right field.

The crowd turned ugly, and the Indians came out of their dugout—to rescue the Rangers. Both teams retreated. Fans started stealing bases and anything else they could get their hands on. Umpires forfeited the game to the Rangers, one of 85 games the Indians lost that year.

"Some might consider the riot started by drunken fans as a black eye for the city," Cleveland native Drew Carey said. "But one of my friends was there and got hit in the head with a bottle and bragged about it for years."

From the Pitcher's Mound to the Broadcast Booth

They called Herb Score the "Howitzer." The lefty mowed down hitters while pitching in the minor leagues in Indianapolis in 1954, leading people to consider him the heir to Bob Feller, who was then closing in on retirement. In Indianapolis, Score went 22–5 and struck out 330 batters.

Score's rookie year of 1955 was one for the books. He won 16 games and struck out 245 batters, a rookie record that stood until Dwight Gooden broke it in 1984. Score was the first rookie to whiff 200 batters since Hall of Famer Grover Cleveland Alexander had done it 44 years earlier. The next year, at age 23, Score won 20 games.

No less a feared hitter than Mickey Mantle called Score the toughest pitcher he ever faced. Ted Williams said Herb Score had the best fastball he'd ever seen, while Bob Feller stood in awe of Score's curveball. Teammate and roommate Rocky Colavito said Herb Score threw more than 100 miles per hour.

Before the 1957 season started, the Red Sox offered to buy Score for $1 million. General manager Hank Greenberg said he wouldn't sell Score at twice the price. Tris Speaker, the manager of the 1920 Indians, said that if nothing happened to Score, he'd be the best ever.

But something did happen. On May 7, 1957, Score was throwing against the Yankees at Municipal Stadium. He got leadoff batter Hank Bauer to ground out to third base. The second batter Score faced was Gil McDougald, who worked the count to 2-and-2. Score fired a fastball, low and away, and McDougald connected to send it back up the middle—and into Score's face.

The ball hit Score in the right eye, and at least one writer said he heard bones breaking from the press box. Score was bleeding but conscious, and he was taken to the clubhouse and then to Lakeside Hospital. He suffered a broken nose, and his cut eyelid was swollen and bleeding. He was done for the season.

Score came back in 1958 and showed flashes of brilliance in spring training. He was the losing pitcher for the Tribe's opener against the Kansas

City Athletics. He picked up his first win of the season in his next start, beating the Tigers in Detroit. He then beat the White Sox, and some people thought he might be all right. He lost two starts to rain, and then pitched against the Senators, with tremendous pain in his throwing elbow. As it turned out, he had ripped a tendon.

Many people believe McDougald's comebacker ended Score's baseball career. But Score himself said it was the elbow injury that finished him. Both sides might be right. Some Indians coaches thought that Score's pitching motion changed after his eye injury, that he was unconsciously recoiling in anticipation of another shot to the head, and that his new mechanics led to his elbow injury.

Score did come back to pitch for the Indians in 1959, and then in 1960 he was traded to the White Sox. His last career win came in 1961, when he threw a two-hitter against the Indians, whose fortunes had fallen as badly as Score's had. He finished his major league playing career with a record of 55–46 and an ERA of 3.36.

Late in the 1963 season, Herb Score became one of the television broadcasters for the Indians. For the following four seasons, he was a TV broadcaster. He then went to the radio broadcast booth, where he stayed for nearly 30 years.

Score became an Cleveland institution. When Nick Mileti bought the Indians, he considered changing the broadcast team before being swamped

with letters demanding he keep Score, whose broadcasts were likened to listening to an old friend.

Score had his own entertainment value. He once
announced that a batter hit a two-hopper that was
picked up by Duane Kuiper on the first bounce.
Some other Herb Score-isms include the following:

- On a fly ball down the line: "Is it fair? Is it foul?
  It is!"

- Signing off: "This is Steve Lamarr, signing off for
  Herb Score. Good night, Tribe fans!"

- Play-by-play: "The pitcher checks the runner on
  first...I beg your pardon, there is no runner
  on first."

- More play-by-play: "Two runs, three hits, one
  error, and after three, we're still scoreless."

Most of Score's years in the broadcast booth were
full of futility for the Indians. Joe Tait, another
Cleveland broadcasting legend who shared time in
the booth with Score, said that nobody in history
had seen more bad baseball than Herb Score. But
Score got to see the Indians rebuild, and then got
to call two Tribe trips to the World Series, in 1995
and 1997.

During the 1997 season, Score announced that he
would retire at the end of the season, and it looked
like the Indians would send him out with a whimper
and not a bang. But the Tribe rallied to take the
American League Central, in no small part because

of the White Sox, who were challenging for the division title, packing it in before the trade deadline.

The Indians dispatched the Yankees in the American League Division Series in five games and faced the Orioles in the American League Championship Series. The O's had knocked the Tribe out of the playoffs the previous year, and Cleveland fans hated Baltimore on principle for having taken away the Browns.

The Tribe split the first two games at Camden Yards. Back in Cleveland, they won two of three games. The Orioles faced elimination when the series returned to Baltimore. Charlie Nagy faced off for the Tribe against Mike Mussina for the Orioles. Neither starter gave up a run, and the game was scoreless into the top of the 11th, when Tony Fernandez hit a home run to give the Indians a 1–0 lead.

Score's emotions got the better of him while calling Fernandez's shot. "And the Indians are going to the World Series!" he said, before composing himself. "Maybe!"

It turned out to be true. The Indians won the game to take the series 4–2 and advance to the World Series. Each of the Indians' wins in the ALCS was a one-run game, a record.

Score called the Indians in the World Series, which ended in heartbreak for Tribe fans, and then he retired. A year later, he was involved in a serious car accident, but he recovered to throw out the first pitch on Opening Day, 1999. Herb Score died in 2008 at his home in Rocky River. But for generations of Indians fans, he remains the voice of summer.

Ohio Baseball Natives

The Rise of the Cyclone

The world knows him as Cy Young, but when he was born in Gilmore in 1867, his parents christened him Denton True Young. "Dent," as his friends liked to call him, was raised on the family farm and left school after the sixth grade to help out with the chores. But like many boys his age, once the chores were done, he would rush over to the local field (usually just an empty field with a diamond shape worn into the grass) with his friends and play their favorite game: baseball.

But baseball became more than just a game for the farm boy. In time, his talent began to surpass that of his friends, and he quickly developed a reputation for his pitching skills, especially his overpowering fastball. Because his devastating fastball destroyed a number of neighborhood fences, he earned the nickname "Cyclone," shortened to Cy.

Too talented to simply play sandlot baseball, Cy Young made the jump to the amateur leagues in the early 1880s before eventually turning pro in 1889, going 15–15 for a Canton team in the Tri-State League. Despite the lackluster record, his pitching style earned him many fans. The Cleveland Spiders of the National League got wind of what the local papers had dubbed the "Canton Cyclone" and made one of the most bizarre trades in the history of baseball: Cy Young was traded to Cleveland for a new suit!

In the next two seasons in Cleveland, Young would establish himself as the team's "money" pitcher as he began his rise to fame as one of the greatest pitchers to ever grace the game of baseball.

The Spiders and the Cyclone moved into National League Park, later shortened to League Park, at East 66th Street and Lexington Avenue, in 1891. The Spiders won a Temple Cup in 1895; however, after a particularly gruesome 1899 season, where they went 20–134, they were eliminated from the National League. Frank and Stanley Robison owned the Spiders and the St. Louis Browns, and they robbed the Spiders of their talent—including Young—for their St. Louis franchise.

In 1900, a new team began play in Cleveland, the Bluebirds—later shortened to Blues because of the color of their uniforms. They played in the American League, then a minor league. The next year, the American League took on major league status, and the Blues were known variously as the Broncos (or Bronchos), the Naps (after player/manager Napoleon Lajoie) and finally, the Indians.

Also in 1901, Young jumped to the American League when he signed with Boston. He played for the Americans—later the Red Sox—until 1909, when he was traded back to Cleveland. He retired from baseball with a career record of 511–316. Both his number of wins and his number of losses are records, and likely ones that will never be broken. Another mark that will probably withstand the test of time is Young's 815 starts. He started 30 or more games in 19 straight seasons. He was inducted into the Baseball Hall of Fame in 1937.

After retiring from baseball, Cy Young returned to the life in Ohio that he had grown up in, working on his farm in Newcomerstown until his death in 1955 at the age of 88. He is buried in Peoli. The following year, an award named for Young was established for the best pitcher in the major leagues. One award was given out annually until 1967, when it was split for American League and National League pitchers.

Hard Luck Harvey

The game was in Milwaukee. The pitcher played for the Pirates. But Harvey Haddix, an Ohio native, is commemorated with a historical marker in his birthplace of Westville in Champaign County for what might be the greatest pitching performance ever.

On May 26, 1959, Haddix was scheduled to start against the Milwaukee Braves, who had won the previous two National League pennants, with a murderer's row that included Hank Aaron, Eddie Mathews and Joe Adcock. The Pirates were without the meat of their lineup, with Dick Groat, Roberto Clemente and Dick Stuart all sitting the game out.

Haddix was a journeyman pitcher and would end up retiring with a 136–113 record. He had spent time in St. Louis, Philadelphia and Cincinnati before arriving in Pittsburgh. He got a pair of World Series wins for the Bucs in the 1960 Fall Classic, but that rainy night in Milwaukee, when he was nursing a cold, was his best performance.

Harvey Haddix threw a perfect game. At the time, he was the seventh pitcher to do so. The problem was that after nine innings, the Pirates hadn't scored a run either. The game went into extras, and Haddix stayed on the mound. He put down the next nine batters he saw—36 up, 36 down.

In the bottom of the 13th, Haddix gave up a chopper to third base by Felix Mantilla. Don Hoak fielded the ball cleanly but pulled first baseman Rocky Nelson off the bag. Mantilla was safe at first on an error. The perfect game was no more.

Mathews bunted, and Mantilla advanced to second. With one out and first base open, Haddix walked Aaron. Joe Adcock came up to bat. He was one of the fiercest power hitters of his day, having set the record for total bases in a game (since eclipsed) with 18, four home runs and a double. Adcock also was the first player to hit a ball into the center field bleachers at the Polo Grounds in New York, a distance of more than 483 feet, and the only person to hit a ball out of Ebbets Field in left field.

Haddix no longer had a perfect game, but he was still throwing a no-hitter. However, he had a history with Adcock. In 1954, when the Braves were playing the Cardinals, Haddix was pitching against

Adcock, who hit a comebacker that cracked Haddix on the knee. Haddix had to change his pitching mechanics because of permanent damage from that line drive, leading Stan Musial to say that he was never the same again.

Adcock stood in against Haddix. On the second pitch, Haddix hung a slider, and Adcock sent it screaming into the night. Mantilla scored. Aaron thought Adcock had hit a ground-rule double, so he touched second and then started running into the dugout. Because Adcock—in his home run trot—passed Aaron on the base path, Adcock was out. The final score ended up being 1–0.

The no-hitter was gone, and Haddix had nothing to show for his performance but a loss. Still, Haddix's achievement is even more incredible when you consider that the Braves had been stealing signs all night and knew what he was throwing.

He ended up turning down TV appearances after the game. He got letters from all over the country, including one from a fraternity at Texas A&M. The letter read simply, "Dear Harvey, Tough shit."

Thurman Munson

Thurman Munson was one of the best players on one of the best teams in the majors. The Yankee catcher was named Rookie of the Year in 1970. He won American League MVP in 1976, when the Yankees advanced to the World Series but were swept by the Big Red Machine. In 1977 and 1978, he was part of the Yankees teams that won back-to-back

World Series. He won three Gold Gloves and was selected to seven All-Star teams. And starting in 1976, he was the Yankees' team captain, the first player on the team so recognized since Lou Gehrig. But like Gehrig, Munson met a tragic end.

Munson was an Ohio boy. He was born in Akron and graduated from Lehman High School in Canton. He attended Kent State University and married his childhood sweetheart. He lived in Canton in the off-season and talked about signing with the Cleveland Indians to be closer to home. He was a nice guy who didn't want people to know it, said former Yankees GM Gabe Paul.

Munson took up flying in 1977 and flew home on off days in season.

On August 2, 1979, a day after playing first base for the Yankees (playing catcher is hard on the knees), Munson was practicing landings in a twin-engine Cessna Citation at Canton-Akron Regional Airport. He was flying with a couple of friends—also pilots—and came in too slowly. The plane started descending faster than he wanted it to, brushing against the tops of the trees near the runway. The plane continued to come down, no longer brushing against trees but hitting them, losing a wing and crashing in a field across the street from the airport.

All three men on board survived the crash, but Munson was trapped. The plane caught fire, and the other two men on the plane escaped, but Munson died from smoke inhalation.

The Yankees were devastated. The team went to Canton for Munson's funeral and returned to Yankee Stadium on August 6 for the Monday-night game against the Orioles. Bobby Murcer hit a three-run home run, and in the ninth inning, his two-run single gave the Yankees a 5–4 win.

Munson's number 15 was immediately retired by the Yankees, and his locker remained vacant and untouched after his death. In fact, his locker was moved to the new Yankee Stadium in 2009 and is now in the stadium's museum.

In 1989, the Indians put their AA farm team in Canton, and a new stadium was built and named for Munson. The Canton-Akron Indians played there until 1996, when they were renamed the Aeros and moved into a new ballpark, Canal Park, in downtown Akron. Thurman Munson Stadium is still used as a venue for high school and college games, as well as by various recreation leagues.

Paul O'Neill and Cosmo Kramer

Columbus native Paul O'Neill had an outstanding career, being selected to the All-Star team five times and winning the World Series five times (once with the Cincinnati Reds and four times with the New York Yankees). But despite those accomplishments, the general public will most likely remember O'Neill from his 1995 appearance on the NBC sitcom *Seinfeld*.

In the episode "The Wink," the character Cosmo Kramer unknowingly sells a birthday card signed by all the members of the Yankees to a sports dealer, and when he needs to retrieve it, he finds out it was given as a gift to a young boy in the hospital. Visiting the boy in the hospital, Kramer makes a deal with the boy that if Paul O'Neill hits two home runs in the game, then the boy will give the birthday card back. Kramer then visits the Yankee locker room and asks Paul O'Neill to hit two home runs. O'Neill responds by saying that hitting home runs is not easy, and then says, "How did you get in here, anyways?" Later in the game, O'Neill manages to hit one home run over the fence and another that is called an inside-the-park home run, but because of an error at third base it is reduced to a triple. Kramer manages to convince the boy to return the card, but with a catch: O'Neill must now catch a fly ball in his hat during the next game.

Although O'Neill's acting career was very short, it certainly was memorable.

How Kevin Youkilis Got His Name

Although Kevin Youkilis was born in Cincinnati, his name would suggest that he was born on a Greek island in the Mediterranean. But his family history actually traces back to a Jewish great-great-great grandfather in Romania.

The story starts in 19th-century Romania. The Cossack majority was not very fond of the Jewish population, and because Romania had a mandatory military service for any male over the age of 16, Kevin Youkilis' great-great-great grandfather, whose family name was originally Weiner, left

Romania and moved to Greece. But after two years abroad, he got homesick and returned to Romania under the name Youkilis to avoid the army and jail for deserting his army duty. The Youkilis family eventually left Romania and found their way to Cincinnati, where Kevin was born in 1979.

Often Youkilis is approached by baseball fans of Greek descent hoping to claim him as one of their own. "People have come up to me and started speaking Greek to me and I don't speak it," Youkilis said. "I feel bad. Ever since I was in Lowell [Class A], people have thought I was Greek. People shout at me, 'I'm Greek, you're Greek.' But I'm not."

As a 14-year-old, Youkilis appeared as an extra in the Melanie Griffth movie *Milk Money*. He even delivered a line. "Let me see the money!" was his introduction to the thespian arts.

Say It Ain't So, Roger!

His career spans more than two decades. He put up numbers that would almost guarantee him a spot in the Baseball Hall of Fame. But did Roger Clemens, a Dayton native, jeopardize it all by taking illegal substances to enhance his already considerable talents?

When Clemens first broke into the majors with the Boston Red Sox in 1984 at the age of 21, his pitching was erratic. Within two years, he had reined in his youthful nerves and found the speed and control that would turn him into one of the most feared pitchers in the league. Through the

1980s, he put up incredible numbers with the Red Sox, hitting the 20-win mark three times and setting league marks in ERA and strikeouts. But in the early 1990s, his numbers showed a marked decline. His win/loss percentage, which peaked at .857 in 1986, had dropped to just .440 in 1993, and his fastball that had once earned him the nickname "Rocket" just didn't seem to have the power it had had in those early years in Boston.

With the downward trend in Clemens' career, the Boston Red Sox didn't re-sign him. He signed with the Toronto Blue Jays in 1997. It was the arrival every Blue Jays fan had been hoping for, and miraculously, the change of cities saw Clemens' numbers skyrocket back to the level of his early Boston days. Many people attributed his return to form to hard work during the off-season.

But then in 2005, Jose Canseco released a book titled *Juiced: Wild Times, Rampant 'Roids, Smash Hits and How Baseball Got Big*. Among Canseco's allegations were that Clemens had expert knowledge of steroids and that he probably had used them after leaving the Red Sox, based on his remarkable improvement in performance.

As Canseco wrote, "One of the benefits of steroids is that they're especially helpful in countering the effects of aging. So in Roger's case, around the time he was leaving the Boston Red Sox—and Dan Duquette, the general manager there, was saying he was 'past his prime'—Roger decided to make some changes. He started working out harder. And whatever else he may have been doing to get stronger, he saw results."

Clemens never directly responded to the steroid allegations made by Canseco, but he did have a response for Canseco, who was habitually in trouble with the law. "I've talked to some friends of his," Clemens said, "and I've teased them that when you're under house arrest and have ankle bracelets on, you have a lot of time to write a book."

The steroid allegations resurfaced in 2006 when Clemens' former personal trainer, Brian McNamee, claimed he had injected Clemens several times with performance-enhancing drugs, beginning in 1998. Clemens vehemently denied the allegations, going on the television program *60 Minutes* and before a Congressional committee to deny the charges. He has continued to deny the charges of steroid use despite a federal grand jury indicting him of making false statements to Congress about his drug use. What will happen in the end to Clemens is still up in the air, but the charges will certainly haunt his legacy and the way he is perceived in the history of baseball.

Ohio Baseball Facts

- In 1908 spring training, the Tigers offered the Indians a trade: the Tribe would give up outfielder Elmer Flick, and the Tigers would give up Ty Cobb. The Indians turned down the deal, saying that Cobb was too much to deal with. Both men went on to Hall of Fame careers, but Cobb's was a little more illustrious, setting records of a .367 life-time batting average and 4191 career hits.

- The first Indians pitcher to win the Cy Young Award was Gaylord Perry in 1972. That season he had a record of 24–16 with an ERA of 1.92. Two other Indians players won the Cy Young: C.C. Sabathia (2007) and Cliff Lee (2008). In his Cy Young season, Lee became the first Tribe pitcher to win more than 20 games since Perry. No pitcher has ever won the Cy Young Award with the Reds.

- Cleveland Municipal Stadium holds many American League and major league attendance records. In 1948, more than 86,000 fans turned out for a World Series game. On September 12, 1954, 86,563 fans turned out to see the Indians play the Yankees. Those attendance records were surpassed in the late 1950s, when the Dodgers, having moved to Los Angeles and awaiting construction of Dodger Stadium, played in the Los Angeles Coliseum, drawing more than 90,000 fans for games. But Municipal Stadium still holds the record for largest attendance at a major league All-Star Game, when 72,086 fans watched Gary Carter hit two home runs and Mike Schmidt (a Dayton native) hit a two-run dinger in the eighth inning of the 1981 Midsummer Classic.

- Municipal Stadium in Cleveland hosted four All-Star Games and holds the top three spots on the list for highest attendance. In addition to the 1981 game, Municipal Stadium hosted the All-Star

Game in 1935, drawing 69,831 fans, and in 1954, drawing 68,751 fans. All told, Cleveland has hosted five All-Star Games, tied with Pittsburgh for third all-time. New York and Chicago—each home to multiple teams—have hosted the game seven times each.

• Pete Rose has the career record for hits with 4256, but when he first broke into the league with the Cincinnati Reds, he went 0 for 11 before finally hitting a triple on April 13, 1963, off Bob Friend of the Pittsburgh Pirates.

• In 1929, Cincinnati Reds announcer Harry Hartman became the first radio personality to use the phrase "Going, going, gone!" whenever the ball was headed for home run territory.

• In 1934, several members of the Cincinnati Reds became the first major league players to fly to a game together. They were flying to a game in Chicago.

• Lee Richmond was born on May 5, 1857, in Sheffield. Richmond was 22 years old when he broke into the big leagues on September 27, 1879, with the Boston Red Caps. On June 12, 1880, pitching against the Cleveland Naps, Richmond became the first pitcher in major league history to throw a perfect game. It was no small feat either, as he had stayed up the night before at a graduation party at Brown University, then played in an early morning baseball game against Yale, then skipped lunch to make the trip out to the ball field to pitch his perfect game.

- Today, no manager would allow his ace pitcher to play more than 30 complete games in one season. In the modern game, there are so many specialized pitchers or relief closers that the average pitcher might complete only a handful of games. But in 1901, Noodles Hahn of the Cincinnati Reds completed an incredible 41 games. Irv Young of the Boston Beaneaters matched him four years later in 1905.

- At a month and a half shy of his 16th birthday, Joe Nuxhall of the Cincinnati Reds became the youngest pitcher to appear in the major leagues when he pitched part of one inning on June 10, 1944, in an 18–0 loss to the St. Louis Cardinals.

- Johnny Burnett of the Cleveland Indians once went 9 for 11 at-bats in an 18-inning marathon game against Philadelphia on July 10, 1932.

- Adam Dunn of the 2004 Cincinnati Reds takes home the dubious distinction of holding the single-season record for the most strikeouts. He whiffed 195 times.

- Cleveland Indians players Nap Lajoie and Harry Bay were the subjects of the first film shot on baseball. The Indians players were filmed fielding and batting for the camera during a postseason exhibition series against Cincinnati in 1903.

- The Cleveland Indians were the first American League team to wear numbers on their uniforms. The practice was not adopted league-wide until some years later.

Ohio Baseball Quotes

"All us Youngs could throw. I used to kill squirrels with a stone when I was a kid, and my granddad once killed a turkey buzzard on the fly with a rock."

—Cy Young

"Too many pitchers, that's all, there are just too many pitchers. Ten or twelve on a team. Don't see how any of them get enough work. Four starting pitchers and one relief man ought to be enough. Pitch 'em every three days and you'd find they'd get control and good, strong arms."

—Cy Young, commenting on modern baseball's use of pitchers

"I was born on the day Lincoln was shot and the *Titanic* sank."

—Pete Rose

"Sliding headfirst is the safest way to get to the next base, I think, and the fastest. You don't lose your momentum, and there's one more important reason I slide headfirst, it gets my picture in the paper."

—Pete Rose

"When you play this game 20 years, go to bat 10,000 times, and get 3000 hits, do you know what that means? You've gone zero for 7000."

–Pete Rose

"He is Cincinnati. He's the Reds."

–Sparky Anderson on Pete Rose

"It isn't the high price of stars that's expensive. It's the high price of mediocrity."

–Bill Veeck, former Indians owner

"That space between the white lines? That's my office. That's where I conduct my business."

–Early Wynn, Indians pitcher and noted knockdown artist

"I never took the game home with me. I always left it in some bar."

–Bob Lemon, Indians pitcher and Yankees manager

"I don't want to embarrass any other catcher by comparing him with Johnny Bench."

–Sparky Anderson

"When a ballplayer is winning, even his sweat smells good."

–Reds pitcher Jim Brosnan

"They ought to change our name to the Cleveland Light Company. We don't have anything but utility men."

—Indians infielder Lou Camilli

"Well, that's football."

—Indians catcher Ray Fosse, after his run-in with Pete Rose at home plate in the 1970 All-Star Game

"I was just in the right place at the right time."

—Cesar Geronimo, who was the 3000th strikeout victim for Bob Gibson in 1974 and Nolan Ryan in 1980

"I knew we were in for a long season when we lined up for the national anthem on opening day and one of my players said, 'Every time I hear that song I have a bad game.'"

—Perrysburg native and well-traveled manager Jim Leyland

Chapter 3

Hockey: The NCAA, the AHL and the NHL

The Original Cleveland Barons

For many years, the Cleveland Barons were regarded as the seventh-best professional hockey team in North America. They were the class of the American Hockey League when there were only the "original six" teams in the National Hockey League: the New York Rangers, Detroit, Chicago, Boston, Montreal and Toronto.

Professional hockey in Cleveland started in 1929 with the International Hockey League (IHL). Harry "Hap" Holmes, a former goalie, relocated the franchise to Cleveland from Hamilton, Ontario. The team was named the Indians. In 1931, there was also an NFL team in Cleveland called the Indians, giving the professional hockey, baseball and football teams in town the same name.

They played at the Elysium, Cleveland's first indoor ice arena, at East 107th Street and Euclid Avenue. The arena was built by Harry Humphrey, the man behind Euclid Beach Park, and billed itself as the largest indoor ice-skating rink in the world.

The Indians hockey team was renamed the Falcons for the 1934–35 season, the same year they were bought by Al Sutphin. They played in the IHL for two more years before they and three other teams in the International Hockey League merged with four teams in the Canadian-American Hockey League to form the International-American Hockey League (IAHL).

In 1937, the Falcons were renamed the Barons, and they moved into what would become their home for almost their entire history: the new Cleveland Arena. The arena, which was modeled after Maple Leaf Gardens in Toronto, seated 9739 people and cost more than $1.5 million.

In 1939, the Barons won the first of their nine Calder Cups, awarded to the IAHL champion, and then, starting in 1940, to the American Hockey League champion. They also won a total of 10 division titles.

The Barons, playing in the largest town not in the NHL, attracted crowds of more than 10,000 for their games, and they were the biggest draw in the league on the road as well. In 1942, the NHL offered admission to the Barons and the Buffalo Bisons of the AHL. By that time, the Barons were outdrawing four of the NHL's seven teams, with an average attendance of 8267 fans. But the AHL was limping along. A team in Philadelphia folded, and World War II was taking men away from teams. So Sutphin stayed in the AHL, for the good of that league.

Sutphin sold the team in 1949 for $2 million (the Browns would only bring $600,000 when Mickey McBride sold them four years later), and in 1952, it appeared that the Barons were set to become the seventh team in the NHL (by then, the New York Americans had folded). But the deal fell through, possibly because of some NHL politicking—there were still some hard feelings from Sutphin's turning them down a decade earlier—but also because the smallest arena in the NHL at the time was the Boston Garden, which seated 14,000 people, 4000 more than the Cleveland Arena could hold.

Cleveland sports impresario Nick Mileti bought the Barons and the arena in 1968 for $2 million (the same price Sutphin sold the team for nearly 20 years earlier), but he too was unsuccessful in getting the NHL to come to Cleveland. After the 1966–67 season, the NHL announced that it would expand to Pittsburgh, St. Louis, Minnesota, Philadelphia, Los Angeles and Oakland. Cleveland was rejected; its arena was still too small.

In 1972, after another bid by Mileti to join the NHL was turned down, he started a World Hockey Association team, the Cleveland Crusaders. The Crusaders played in the arena at the same time the Barons did, but after the 1973–74 season, the Crusaders moved to Mileti's newest creation, the Richfield Coliseum, located 25 miles outside of Cleveland. During the 1973–74 season, the Barons were relocated by Mileti to Florida. In 1976, the Crusaders were moved to the Twin Cities to make way for the NHL, which had finally come to Cleveland.

The NHL in Cleveland

Before NHL hockey could come to Ohio, first it had to fail in Oakland. The Seals came into existence during the league's first big expansion in 1967. The team entered the NHL as the California Seals, but just two months into their first season, the team changed its name to the Oakland Seals to pay tribute to the city they called home.

The NHL knew that they were taking a risk moving into a city that was not known for its hockey community, but from the outset the team was plagued with poor attendance and a horrible performance on the ice. After a few growing pains, the Seals managed to make the playoffs twice. The franchise battled through low attendance, threats of relocation, changes in ownership and losing seasons before finally succumbing to financial pressures in 1976. Owner Melvin Swig then packed the team's bags and moved operations to Cleveland for the start of the 1976–77 season, after being persuaded to do so by minority owner George Gund, a Cleveland native.

The team was named the Barons, after the old AHL team. It was hoped that by moving the team to a city with a population more knowledgeable about hockey, the NHL might be able to salvage the franchise. The Barons played at Richfield Coliseum, which at the time was the largest venue in the NHL, seating 18,544 fans.

The season began without much fanfare; barely 9000 fans showed up for the team's home opener on October 7, 1976. The Barons seemed doomed from the start. Of the 40 home games they played that season, only seven drew more than 10,000 fans. Support was also lacking in the team's bank account, as an expensive lease with the Coliseum nearly caused the team to fold in January of their first season. The Barons even missed payroll twice in February and had to secure a loan from the NHL and the Players Association just to finish out the rest of the schedule.

By the end of the season, Swig had given up any hopes of making money with the Barons and sold his stake of the franchise to Gordon and George Gund. The brothers poured dollars into the team, hoping that money could fix their issues, and the team's fortunes on the ice seemed to mirror the security in the front office.

The Barons opened the 1977–78 season in mediocre fashion, winning just as many games as they lost, but during a home game against the Montreal Canadiens on November 23, it seemed that their fortunes were turning for the better. The Barons managed to beat Montreal, a feat accomplished just nine other times that season. In January, the Barons reeled off wins against NHL powers Toronto, the New York Islanders and Buffalo. Cleveland then fought the Philadelphia Flyers to a 2–2 tie, and by February, sports fans in the city began talking of making the playoffs. But the bottom fell out later that month when the team went on a 15-game losing streak and dropped from playoff contention.

After the disastrous end to the season, there was no way the Barons could survive another year of poor attendance and high rents. The Gund brothers tried unsuccessfully to buy the Coliseum. But lucky for them, the Minnesota North Stars were in equally dire straits, so in order for both teams to save face, the league granted approval for the two franchises to merge. They would remain the Minnesota North Stars but assume the Barons' place in the Adams Division, and just like that, NHL hockey had come and gone in Ohio and would not return until 22 years later with the arrival of the Columbus Blue Jackets.

The Columbus Blue Jackets

For many years, Columbus was the largest city in the U.S. without a professional major league sports team. Then, in 2000, the NHL expanded, granting new teams to Columbus and to Minnesota to replace the North Stars, which had moved to Dallas.

The Columbus Blue Jackets owe their name to the great tradition and military history of Ohio. During the Civil War, Ohio played a key role in providing the Union army with troops, military officers and supplies. Several leading generals hailed from Ohio, including Ulysses S. Grant, William T. Sherman and Philip H. Sheridan. Although portions of southern

Ohio had allied themselves with the Confederate cause, Ohio, along with its governor, David Tod, was one of the biggest supporters of Abraham Lincoln. And when the president requested that Ohio raise 10 regiments at the outbreak of the war, the state responded by raising 23 regiments. The blue jackets of the Union army were a common sight during the war, and Columbus itself hosted several large military bases.

So when it came time to name Columbus's new hockey team in 2000, it was an easy choice for the owners of the club to choose the name Blue Jackets. The team's alternate logo for a period was a Union Civil War cap with crossed hockey sticks on the front of the cap instead of the crossed swords or guns found on original Civil War caps. From 2000 to 2004, the club's other alternate logo was a yellow jacket wasp dressed in a Union Civil War blue jacket holding a stick. It's unclear why the yellow jacket wasp was used to promote a team named after the state's proud Civil War tradition.

Rick Nash Goes to Columbus

In 2002, Rick Nash sat in the Air Canada Centre in Toronto surrounded by family and friends, waiting to hear his name called in the NHL Entry Draft. He had been reading the hockey pages for days as pundits bantered back and forth as to who would be selected first overall. The Florida Panthers had the first selection, followed by the Atlanta Thrashers, and then the Columbus Blue Jackets. Most pundits had Medicine Hat Tigers defenseman

Jay Bouwmeester pegged as the number one pick to go to Florida, and so had Rick Nash. Why wouldn't he believe them? He was not even 18 years old yet; what did he know about the business of hockey?

But what Nash forgot was that a few days earlier during an interview with Blue Jackets general manager Doug MacLean, he had said something that would direct him to a team on draft day. "I'd love to have you," MacLean told Nash, "but I don't know if I'm going to get you at number three." To which Nash smartly replied, "Well, why don't you go get me?" Sitting at the draft a few days after the interview, Nash had all but forgotten about the conversation, but MacLean took the teenager's brazen advice seriously.

Up until draft day, Panthers general manager Rick Dudley had openly coveted defenseman Jay Bouwmeester. But come draft day, MacLean had heard rumblings that Dudley had begun to waver. MacLean was also banking on Atlanta Thrashers general manager Don Waddell taking top prospect Kari Lehtonen to fill a need for a franchise goaltender. But with Dudley's indecision weighing heavily, MacLean did not want to take the risk of losing Nash. He decided to make a bold move minutes before the Panthers were slated to pick.

MacLean approached the Panthers' table on the floor of the Air Canada Centre and offered the Blue Jackets' pick at number three and the option to swap picks with the Jackets in 2003. Dudley snapped up the deal after sending Waddell a pair of late-round picks to ensure that he didn't select

Bouwmeester, and MacLean now had the number one pick.

All the while the deals were being hashed out, Rick Nash sat in the stands expecting to be selected later rather than sooner, and then NHL commissioner Gary Bettman approached the microphone to announce a trade.

"I was sitting there just thinking about Bouwmeester going first to Florida and the next thing you hear there's been a trade," Nash said. "My stomach just dropped...it was like going on a big roller coaster."

Doug MacLean then walked to the podium with a few other members of the Columbus Blue Jackets and announced that Rick Nash was the number one pick of the 2002 NHL Entry Draft. The entire Nash family jumped out of their seats with joy. Nash walked over to MacLean and smiled, shook his hand and put on the Blue Jackets jersey.

For MacLean, he saw his bold draft-day trade as a necessity if he wanted to get any sleep that night, and for the rest of his professional life, for that matter. "I haven't said it very often," MacLean said later, "but I would have been sick to my stomach leaving the draft without him."

Tragedy Strikes Nationwide Arena

Brittanie Cecil of West Alexandria was an avid Blue Jackets fan and loved to watch them play on TV. But just before the Calgary Flames were set to visit

Columbus on March 16, 2002, her dad surprised her with an early 14th-birthday gift: two tickets behind the Columbus goal to watch the game.

Arriving at the game and taking their seats behind the net, Brittanie and her father sat happily and watched their favorite team. With 12:18 left in the second period, a shot by Columbus Blue Jackets center Espen Knutsen was deflected by Calgary Flames defenseman Derek Morris. The puck flew up into the stands and struck Brittanie in the head.

The game carried on, as the players and referees were completely unaware that anyone had been injured. In fact, Brittanie did not appear to be in any danger at first and simply walked with her father to the first aid station. It was only later at the Columbus Children's Hospital that a scan revealed that she had suffered a skull fracture. Once admitted to the hospital, Brittanie suffered a seizure, but the next day she appeared to have recovered without any complaints of pain or dizziness.

However, a CT scan had failed to reveal a tear in her vertebral artery, resulting in a severe swelling in her brain. On March 18, Brittanie developed a high fever and lost consciousness. She died a few hours later, 48 hours after being struck with the puck. Columbus Blue Jackets general manager Doug MacLean attended the funeral and spoke on behalf of the organization.

For the remainder of the season, the Blue Jackets wore a sticker on their helmets with Brittanie's initials. The two players involved in her death still have not forgotten.

"You try to say, 'It happens all the time,' but you can't," Derek Morris said. "I don't know how many times pucks get deflected over the glass, but it doesn't make it any better. You can always say, 'It's not my fault,' but you always feel like it is, a little."

"I think about it all the time," said Knutsen. "It was a terrible accident, and I cannot get it off my mind."

As a result of Brittanie's death, at the beginning of the next season the NHL implemented mandatory netting at both ends of the rink in every arena to protect fans from pucks. Hers was the first death of a fan in the history of the NHL.

The Cannon

In an attempt to bring more fans to the arena and make the spectators' hockey experience more enjoyable, the Columbus Blue Jackets organization brought into the arena a replica of an 1857 Napoleonic cannon prior to the start of the 2007–08 season. It is fired at home games every time the Jackets take the ice at the start of a game, score a goal or win the game. Other stadiums use large air horns or blast music when a team scores, so why not a replica Napoleonic cannon? Makes sense to me!

Go Falcons!

In 1963, hockey started as a club sport on the campus of Bowling Green State University (BGSU).

Six years later, after the construction of a $1.8-million ice arena on campus, the Falcons competed as a varsity team in the Midwest Collegiate Hockey Association, finishing in top spot in their first year in the league. In 1971, the Falcons became inaugural members of the Central Collegiate Hockey Association (CCHA). They won league tournaments in 1973, 1977, 1978 and 1979 and won league titles in 1976, 1978 and 1979.

As the 1980s dawned, BGSU was a hockey powerhouse. Ken Morrow and Mark Wells, roommates at BGSU, were on the "Miracle on Ice" men's hockey team that won the gold medal at the 1980 Olympics. The Falcons continued to win the CCHA, in 1982, 1983 and 1984, a year in which BGSU was able to claim a share of Olympic gold again, this time won by figure skater and alumnus Scott Hamilton.

The Falcons had lost three games in the 1984 CCHA Tournament, but on the strength of their 30-win season, they advanced to the NCAA Tournament. There, they dropped a 6–3 game to Boston University. They won a rematch 4–1, but the two teams were tied in total goals at seven. They played an overtime period to decide who would advance, and BGSU won to advance to the semifinals. The Falcons beat Michigan State 2–1 in the semifinals to advance to the finals against the University of Minnesota-Duluth—at Lake Placid.

BGSU drew first blood, but they were trailing 3–1 by the time the third period started. With 1:47 left to play, the Falcons tied the game at four, and the game went into the first of four overtime periods.

With 2:49 left in the fourth overtime, Dan Kane passed the puck to Gino Cavallini, who backhanded it into the net for Bowling Green's first and only national title. The Falcons were the first team in the CCHA to win a national title, and the game remains the longest NCAA Division I championship game ever played.

Ohio Hockey Facts

- Despite the Oakland Golden Seals' bad record and the Cleveland Barons' even worse record, the franchise never fired head coach Jack Evans, who was with the Seals for six seasons and the Barons for two.

- In their two seasons in the NHL, the Cleveland Barons had only one player who scored more than 30 goals in a season. Dennis Maruk scored 36 goals during the 1977–78 season. He had scored 28 goals during the 1976–77 season.

- Bruce Gardiner scored the Columbus Blue Jackets' first goal on October 7, 2000, in a 5–3 loss to the Chicago Blackhawks.

- Defenseman Lyle Odelein was the first captain of the Columbus Blue Jackets.

- In 2004, Rick Nash shared the Rocket Richard Trophy with Jarome Iginla and IIya Kovalchuk for the most goals in the season, with 41.

- NHL trophies won by members of the Columbus Blue Jackets: Rocket Richard Trophy, Rick Nash, 2003–04; and Calder Memorial Trophy, Steve Mason, 2008–09.

Ohio Hockey Quotes

"They didn't throw me on one of the top lines, but they didn't keep me out as a healthy scratch, either. I think Dave King and Doug [MacLean] were using me well, and I think it was good development for me. I couldn't think of a better team to come to for a young guy than Columbus. You aren't just going to jump in and be a star player at 18. It's tough to be a star in the NHL. I just fit in and played my role on the third line, and just kind of hit and chipped in with a goal here or there when I could."

–Rick Nash

"He's a big part of our future and we think he has a chance to make an impact on our team as early as this season."

–Blue Jackets general manager Doug MacLean on a young Rick Nash

"He's as tough as they come. All I know he may be the best-conditioned athlete in the league, and that's a pretty good start. There's not a team in the NHL that wouldn't like to have Adam Foote, I can tell you that."

–GM Doug MacLean on defenseman Adam Foote

Chapter 4

Basketball: High School Phenoms, College Legends, a King and a Big O

The Birth of the NBA

The National Basketball Association was born in 1949 from a merger of two professional basketball leagues: the National Basketball League and the Basketball Association of America.

The National Basketball League was a series of Midwestern and Great Lakes–area teams, many sponsored by various companies. The Fort Wayne Pistons (now the Detroit Pistons) were named for a product made by their sponsor. The Pistons, Minneapolis Lakers, Rochester Royals and Buffalo Bisons are still active in the NBA today. The Lakers moved to Los Angeles, the Royals are now the Sacramento Kings, and the Bisons are the Atlanta Hawks. In Ohio, the NBL had teams in Dayton, Columbus, Cleveland, Cincinnati, Toledo and Youngstown. The Youngstown Bears counted among their alumni Press Maravich, who went on to become a successful high school and college coach. His son, Pete Maravich, would become arguably the greatest college basketball player ever at Louisiana State University.

The Basketball Association of America started in 1946. Its 11 teams included the Cleveland Rebels, owned by Al Sutphin, who also owned the Cleveland Barons hockey team and the Cleveland Arena, home of the Rebels and the Barons. The Rebels went 30–30, but folded after a year. In 1948, the Pistons, Lakers and Royals jumped from the NBL to the BAA, and in 1949, the two circuits merged with a total of 17 teams—none of which were Ohio teams.

The Rise of the Royals

In 1957, the Royals moved from Rochester, New York, to Cincinnati, becoming the first NBA team in Ohio. The Royals were bankrupt, and at the time, the NBA draft included a provision where teams could forfeit their first-round picks to draft local players. The move was made to allow the NBA to build up a local following by drafting local, and presumably popular, players. The Royals used territorial picks to their advantage. The University of Cincinnati had the most territorial picks in the NBA, with three players—most notably Oscar Robertson—going to the Royals. Jerry Lucas, a Middletown High School graduate who played at Ohio State University, was also a Royals territorial pick.

The Royals were able to put a strong team on the court, including local picks Lucas, Robertson, Wayne Embry and Jack Twyman. But they played in the formidable NBA East, and the Boston Celtics dynasty of the 1950s and 1960s always stood in the way for the Royals.

One of the reasons the Royals moved from Rochester to Cincinnati was that the Queen City of the Midwest had no football team to compete with for attention from fans. That changed with the arrival of the Bengals in 1968, and the Royals began playing "home" games throughout Ohio, in Columbus, Dayton and Cleveland. Attendance declined, and the Cavaliers' arrival in Cleveland helped force the Royals' move to Kansas City in 1972.

The Roy Campanella of the NBA

Maurice Stokes was on his way to becoming one of the greatest basketball players of his day, possibly of all time. But a freak accident derailed his career and his life, turning his story into a tragic tale.

Stokes grew up in the Pittsburgh area. He went to St. Francis College (now St. Francis University) in Loretto, near Altoona. In 1955, he was named National Invitational Tournament MVP—when the NIT was a bigger deal than the NCAA Tournament.

Everyone wanted him, and the Rochester Royals drafted him second overall in the NBA draft. He was named Rookie of the Year, and Bob Cousy said later on that Stokes was the first modern power forward.

Cousy's coach, Red Auerbach, said Stokes was Magic Johnson before Magic Johnson.

But in the last regular-season game of the 1957–58 season, Stokes was injured. He fell to the floor during a game against the Lakers in Minneapolis on March 12, 1958, and was knocked unconscious. He was revived with smelling salts and returned to the game. He played again in the Royals' playoff opener three days later, when they lost to the Pistons, but he was sick on the flight back to Cincinnati.

Stokes went into a coma. When the season ended, the Royals were sold for $200,000. If Stokes ever played again, the sale price would rise to $225,000.

Stokes emerged from his coma, but he was paralyzed and couldn't speak. The diagnosis was post-traumatic encephalopathy. The fall had injured his brain. Stokes worked arduously to try to regain movement and to communicate with others.

Jack Twyman, a teammate with the Royals, made it his mission to help Stokes. He got himself named Stokes' guardian, and he started an all-star exhibition game in Stokes' honor to help with medical expenses. The Maurice Stokes Game was played annually in Monticello, New York, until 2000, when, because of liability concerns, it became the Maurice Stokes/Wilt Chamberlain Celebrity Golf Pro-Am.

In 1969, the athletic center at St. Francis was named the Stokes Center. Maurice Stokes died in 1970 of a heart attack, at 36 years old. He is buried at St. Francis.

The Big O

Indiana's loss was Ohio's gain when it came to Oscar Robertson.

Robertson went to Crispus Attucks High School, an all-black high school in Indianapolis. At the time, Indiana had a single high school basketball championship. As a sophomore, Robertson and Attucks lost a tournament game to Milan High School, which went on to win the state title and form the basis for the movie *Hoosiers*. But in each of the next two years, Attucks won the state title, becoming the first all-black high school to win a state title.

Robertson wanted desperately to go to college and play basketball at Indiana. But he ended up at the University of Cincinnati, where he was the second black athlete ever at the school. Robertson was named an All-American and led two Bearcats teams to the Final Four. When he graduated college, he had the highest average points per game in NCAA history, a record since broken by Pete Maravich. Robertson also co-captained (with Jerry West) the 1960 Olympic basketball team, which won the gold medal in Rome.

The Royals picked Robertson as a territorial pick in 1960, and he was named the NBA Rookie of the

Year in 1961. And the next year, Robertson, a point guard, did something unparalleled in NBA history. In the 1961–62 season, he averaged 30.5 points, 12.5 rebounds and 11.4 assists, becoming the only player in the history of the league to average a triple-double for an entire season. He almost did it again in 1963–64, averaging 9.9 assists per game to go with 30.3 points and 10.4 rebounds in an MVP season.

Before the 1970–71 season, Robertson was dealt by the Royals to the Milwaukee Bucks, where he was paired with a young center named Lew Alcindor (later Kareem Abdul-Jabbar). That year, the Bucks were the best team in the NBA, blowing through the regular season and playoffs and finishing with a sweep of the Baltimore Bullets to win the title.

The Royals were renamed the Kings after the 1972 move to Kansas City. They retired Robertson's number, as did Milwaukee. Robertson was a 1980 inductee into the Basketball Hall of Fame, and in 1996, he was named one of the NBA's 50 all-time greatest players.

The Cleveland Pipers

In the span of two years, the Cleveland Pipers went from a nearly bankrupt semi-pro team to the brink of joining the NBA—thanks to their owner, George Steinbrenner.

Steinbrenner bought the team, with help from his friends, for $25,000 in paying off the team's debts and whatever operating budget they needed for the 1961–62 season. His father, Henry Steinbrenner, wouldn't lend George any money to buy the team. Among Steinbrenner's investors was a Detroit sportsman who made his money in trucking: Ralph Wilson. He also owned a share of the Detroit Lions until 1959, when he sold it to buy into the new American Football League. Wilson has owned the Buffalo Bills ever since, and their home stadium in Orchard Park, New York, bears his name.

The Pipers played in the National Industrial Basketball League from 1959 to 1961, but went on to join the American Basketball League, a circuit founded in 1961 by Abe Saperstein, the original owner and promoter of the Harlem Globetrotters.

That year, they won the first half of the season and played the second-half winners, the Kansas City Steers, for the league championship. The Pipers won the final series three games to two to be American Basketball League champions in the league's only full season of operation.

But the Pipers finished the season, in addition to being league champions, in debt to the tune of $240,000. They drafted Jerry Lucas, the Middletown native who became one of the greatest college basketball players of all time at Ohio State University, but had to pay the Cincinnati Royals, who had territorial rights for the state of Ohio.

In 1962, the Pipers were invited to become the 10th team in the NBA. The only problem? The team, already awash in red ink, had to come up with $250,000 for the franchise rights. Steinbrenner couldn't come up with the money, and the deal came and went.

The local press excoriated Steinbrenner. An editorial in the *Cleveland Press* suggested that he had wrecked any chance Cleveland had at eventually becoming an NBA city. Of course, that turned out not to be true.

The Birth of the Cavs

As an alumnus of Bowling Green State University, Nick Mileti was roped into promoting a men's basketball game between BGSU and Niagara University at Cleveland Arena. He sold 11,000 tickets for the game on December 14, 1967. "I figured if I could get 11,000 one night, I could draw 8000 every night," Mileti said.

The next year, Mileti bought the arena and its tenants, the Cleveland Barons hockey team. In 1968, there were 14 teams in the NBA, and some reports indicated that all but two finished in the red. The Cincinnati Royals even played a few "home" games in Cleveland. But Mileti still wanted to be a part of it, and in 1970, Cleveland, along with Buffalo and Portland, was awarded a franchise. Jerry Tomko (the father of Reds pitcher Brett) submitted the winning entry for the team's name. They would be called the Cavaliers. Mileti, a good Cleveland boy, made their original colors wine and gold—the same colors as his alma mater, John Adams High School.

Bill Fitch—who coached Bowling Green the night the Cleveland Arena hosted them—would be the Cavaliers' first coach. His beginning was an inauspicious one. The Cavaliers dropped their first 14 games before getting a win, and then lost the next 12. All told, they finished 15–67 in their first season.

By 1972, the Cavs had Ohio all to themselves. The Royals left for Kansas City and were renamed the Kings, since Kansas City already had a team named the Royals. The Kings would play some home games in Omaha, as well, before moving in 1985 to Sacramento.

The Miracle of Richfield

The Cavaliers had an eminently forgettable first season—one sportswriter bestowed the nickname "Cadavers" on them. Then they started making deals to build the nucleus of a good team.

In 1971, the Cavaliers drafted Austin Carr out of Notre Dame. In 1973, they drafted Jim Brewer, and the next year, they took Campy Russell and Clarence "Foots" Walker. They also traded for Jim Chones from the Lakers in 1974, and picked up Dick Snyder, a Canton native, from the SuperSonics.

The Cavs started out of the gate slowly in the 1975–76 season, so they traded for one of the all-time greats, who still had a little left in the tank:

Akron native and BGSU All-American, Nate Thurmond. Thurmond came off the bench and played some key minutes for the Cavaliers; he sparked them to a 43–22 record after coming to Cleveland. Overall, they finished 49–33 and won their first division title. It was also their first playoff appearance and first winning record.

In the first round of the playoffs, the Cavaliers would see the Washington Bullets, who finished a game behind Cleveland in the Central Division. The Bullets had talent such as Hall of Famers Elvin Hayes, Wes Unseld and Dave Bing, who went on to be elected mayor of Detroit.

By this time, the Cavaliers had moved out of the Cleveland Arena and into the Coliseum in Richfield, a town off Interstate 71 about 20 miles from Cleveland and 10 miles from Akron. Mileti reasoned that the Coliseum, which opened with a concert by Frank Sinatra in 1974, would draw Cavs fans from throughout northeastern Ohio.

For the first game of the best-of-seven series, the Coliseum was rocking. But the Bullets put a damper on festivities, getting an early lead and holding on for a 100–95 win. The second game went to the Capital Centre, where Bingo Smith hit a midrange jumper with two seconds to play to give the Cavs an 80–79 win. The Cavaliers won game three, in Richfield, 88–76. Austin Carr scored 17 points. Game four went back to Maryland, and the Bullets tied the series with a 109–98 win.

Bullets owner Abe Pollin said, "Those bastards aren't going to win another game."

And it looked like he might be right. With 10 seconds left in game five, more than 21,000 people were shouting themselves hoarse at the Coliseum. Bill Fitch was trying to scream over the din, yelling to foul someone. Elvin Hayes went to the line for the Bullets, up 91–90. He missed both shots. Smith tried to take the winning shot—and launched an air ball. Jim Cleamons took the ball and laid it in for a 92–91 Cavaliers win.

The Bullets took a 17-point lead in game six and blew it, but they still held on for an overtime 102–98 win to set up game seven. Once again, it would come down to the wire. The Cavs and Bullets were tied at 85 points with nine seconds to play, and the Cavs had the ball. Dick Snyder faked inside and put up a shot to give the Cavaliers an 87–85 lead. Elvin Hayes couldn't take a pass, so Phil Chenier threw up a desperation baseline shot as time expired. He missed. The Cavaliers took the series. Bedlam ensued.

The Cavaliers were headed to the Eastern Conference finals to face the Boston Celtics, who were just two years removed from their 12th NBA Championship. The Celtics were getting older, but they still had John Havlicek (a Bridgeport High School graduate who went on to play basketball at Ohio State—and was drafted by the Browns) and future coaches Don Nelson and Paul Silas (who would serve as LeBron James' first coach with the Cavs).

The Celtics also had younger players like Charlie Scott, Dave Cowens and Jo Jo White.

But two days before the series was to start, disaster struck: Jim Chones went up to block a shot in practice and came down with a broken metatarsal bone in his foot. He would watch the series on crutches. Chones was the team's leading scorer, and second on the team in rebounding.

The Cavs put up a good fight and took the series to six games, but the Celtics prevailed and went on to win their 13th NBA Championship, dispatching the Phoenix Suns in six games.

The Stepien Rule

In 1980, the Cavaliers were sold to Ted Stepien, a Pittsburgh native who moved to Cleveland and made his money in advertising. His name would become synonymous with front-office incompetence, to the point where the NBA stepped in.

Stepien's first order of business with the Cavs? Find cheerleaders. He named them the Teddi Bears, after his youngest daughter, Teddi. He hired Bill Musselman, a man known to Ohio basketball fans for coaching a University of Minnesota team that decided to start a brawl on the court against Ohio State. Stepien then tried to take Nick Mileti's idea of regionalization a little further; he wanted to call the team the Ohio Cavaliers, and have them play games in Columbus, Pittsburgh and Buffalo.

Stepien also was not enamored with Joe Tait, the man who'd been the radio voice of the Cavaliers since the team's inception, and a Cleveland sportscasting legend (Tait also was a radio and television broadcaster for the Indians for 15 years). Stepien said Tait should be more supportive of the Cavaliers, and not criticize so much. At the end of the 1980–81 season, Tait left Cleveland. He spent a year in exile in New Jersey and another as the television voice of the Chicago Bulls before coming back to the Cavs. The biggest crowd of the 1980–81 season came out for the final home game, not to honor the Cavs, but to cheer on Joe Tait in his last game before leaving. In fact, that night was the only sellout in Stepien's tenure as owner of the Cavaliers. Stepien went on to fire several employees simply because of their relationship with Tait.

The Cavs went 28–54 in 1980–81, Stepien's first year owning the club. But that was just a warmup for a dreadful 1981–82 season, when the Cavaliers—once again earning the moniker of "Cadavers"—stunk up the joint with a 15–67 record, the same as their expansion year.

That year, the Cavs had four coaches: general manager Don Delaney, who filled in for Mussleman after Stepien fired him; Bob Kloppenburg, an assistant who served as head coach for a game after Delaney was relieved of coaching duties; Chuck Daly, who was in his first head coaching job and would later go on to win back-to-back NBA titles with the Detroit Pistons; and Mussleman, who was brought back after Daly was fired.

During Stepien's three-year reign, the Cavaliers also had a bad habit of dealing their first-round draft picks for players of varying—usually poor—quality. At one point, the Dallas Mavericks had been given Cleveland's first-round picks in 1983, 1984, 1985 and 1986, prompting Mavs coach Dick Motta to say, "I was afraid to go to lunch for fear I'd miss a call from Cleveland."

On November 6, 1980, the league stepped in. Commissioner Larry O'Brien told all the NBA teams that league operations director Joe Axelson would approve any trades with Cleveland. The league then changed its bylaws, adopting what is now called the Stepien Rule, which states that no team can trade away first-round draft picks in consecutive years.

In 1983, because of low attendance, Stepien mulled over the idea of moving the Cavaliers to Toronto and calling them the Toronto Towers. Instead, he sold the Cavaliers to brothers George and Gordon Gund, who had purchased the Coliseum two years earlier. The Gunds bought the Cavaliers and Stepien's business, Nationwide Advertising, for $20 million. They also went back to the NBA and got bonus first-round draft picks from 1983 to 1986, in return for payments to the league.

All told, the Cavaliers went 66–180 during the three seasons that Stepien owned the team. They also lost an estimated $15 million—and untold amounts of respect.

The Shot

By 1988, the Cavaliers had reversed fortunes. Thanks to some shrewd deals by new general manager Wayne Embry, the Cavs had put a team together that could challenge not just for a division title but also for the NBA title.

Brad Daugherty, a center out of North Carolina, was drafted. The Mavericks traded Mark Price to the Cavs for a second-round pick and $50,000. And the Cavs were able to draft John "Hot Rod" Williams, whose draft stock dropped because of alleged involvement with point-shaving at Tulane (he was exonerated).

Lenny Wilkens was the Cavs' coach. He had played briefly for the Cavs from 1972 to 1974, and he coached the Seattle SuperSonics to their only NBA title in 1979.

Magic Johnson said the Cavaliers were poised to be the team of the 1990s, and they were a good team for the rest of Wilkens' tenure as Cavs coach. But there was always someone better, and that someone was Michael Jordan and the Bulls.

In 1988–89, the Cavs won a franchise-record 57 games, and finished second in the Central Division behind the "Nasty Boy" Pistons, coached by former Cavs coach Chuck Daly and featuring former Cavalier Bill Laimbeer. Price, Daugherty and Larry Nance were All-Stars.

The Cavs got the Bulls in the first round of the playoffs. They split the first two games before a decisive game five at Richfield on May 7, 1989. The Cavs were up 100–99 with three seconds left. Brad Sellers threw the in-bounds pass to Jordan, who jumped up, shot—and scored over Craig Ehlo. The Bulls won, 101–100, and the Cavs went home for the summer. For the second year in a row, the Bulls had eliminated the Cavs.

In 1990, the Cavs lost in the first round of the playoffs to the Philadelphia 76ers. They failed to make the playoffs in 1991, and in 1992, the Cavs found themselves in the NBA Eastern Conference finals for just the second time in team history, facing, yep, you guessed it, the Bulls.

The Bulls blew out the Cavs, four games to two. They swept the Cavs out of the playoffs again the next year, and Wilkens resigned as coach. He was succeeded by Mike Fratello, but the results were the same: the Cavs lost to the Bulls in three straight games in the first round of the 1994 play-offs. Fratello coached the Cavs for six years and won a total of two playoff games, compared with 12 losses.

The Cavs moved into Gund Arena in downtown Cleveland, across the street from Jacobs Field, the new home of the Indians, in 1994. But the move coincided with a slide toward irrelevance—which would

not be halted until a high school phenom from
Akron arrived.

Mr. Basketball

LeBron James made a stunning decision: to play
basketball with his friends. He was called a traitor.
He was called a sellout. He was in eighth grade.

James decided to go to St.Vincent–St. Mary High
School (STVM), a Catholic school in Akron. While
still in junior high, he had demonstrated his tran-
scendent basketball abilities playing for an AAU
team called the Shooting Stars. He and other members of the team wanted to continue playing
basketball together. It seemed a foregone conclu-
sion that they'd go to Buchtel High School, one of
seven public schools in Akron; after all, Buchtel's
student population was about 97 percent minority.
However, James and his teammates wanted to go
someplace where they could make an immediate
impact. STVM had a minority population of about
13 percent and was not regarded as a basketball
powerhouse.

When James arrived at STVM in 1999, he became
the king of the school and turned the Fighting Irish
into one of the best boys basketball teams in the
country. As a freshman, he started and led
the team with an average of 21 points and 6.2
rebounds per game. The Irish cruised to a 23–1
record, all the way to the Division III state title. In his
sophomore year, James averaged 25.2 points and
7.2 rebounds per game, and the Fighting Irish

again only lost once all season and won the state title. James was named Ohio's Mr. Basketball, the first sophomore so recognized by the Associated Press. By this time, LeBron James was known throughout Ohio, and word of his talents began to spread even farther.

As a junior, James averaged 30 points and 8.3 rebounds per game, but despite his heroics on the basketball court, the Fighting Irish did not repeat as state champions. They were bumped up to Division II because of enrollment, and lost in the finals to the Roger Bacon High School out of Cincinnati.

After the season was over, James, then 17, felt he was ready to make the jump to the NBA. But the league had a rule that said all prospective players must complete high school to be eligible. James unsuccessfully petitioned for an adjustment to the NBA rules. By then, most people in Ohio had heard of the kid who repeated as Mr. Basketball, but the sudden popularity of James—including requests for appearances on David Letterman and Regis and Kelly's TV shows—forced his team out of St. Vincent's gym and into the Rhodes Arena on the campus of the University of Akron to accommodate the media and fans clamoring to get a peek at the next Michael Jordan. One regular-season game against high school power Mater Dei was held in Pauley Pavilion in Los Angeles. Even NBA stars like Shaquille O'Neal attended some games, and ESPN carried STVM games nationwide.

Despite all the distractions, the Fighting Irish once again finished at the top of their league and took home the Division II state championship, beating Kettering Archbishop Alter. The moment James finished high school, he entered into the NBA draft, and the lucky winner of the LeBron James sweepstakes was the Cleveland Cavaliers.

The Cavs Get the King

In 1998, the Cavs finished the season 47–35 and qualified for the playoffs. They lost 3–1 to the Indiana Pacers. After that, the Cavs sank into oblivion. In each of the next five seasons, they didn't win more than 32 games. The Cavs' nadir came in the 2002–03 season, when Ricky Davis put up a shot at the wrong basket to try to get a rebound for a triple-double (it didn't count). But the silver lining in the Cavs' 17–65 record that year was that it made them a lottery pick. The ping-pong ball bounced their way, and they got the first pick in the draft.

Of course, they picked LeBron James. *Sports Illustrated* went so far as to say that he was the savior delivered to them like Moses. James lived up to his billing almost immediately. In the 2003–04 season, the Cavs had an 18-game improvement, to 35 wins. James was the Rookie of the Year. The next year, the Cavs went 42–40, and spring 2006 brought the Cavs' first playoff appearance since 1998. All James did in his playoff debut was get a triple-double, the first player to do that since Magic Johnson. The Cavs advanced to the Eastern

Conference semis and took the Pistons to seven games before falling.

The following year, the Cavs advanced to the Eastern Conference finals for the third time in team history, against the Pistons. This time, James and the Cavs wouldn't be denied. In game five at the Palace of Auburn Hills, James scored 48 points, including the Cavs' last 25 points, in a double-overtime win. The Cavs returned to Cleveland and beat the Pistons to clinch their first appearance in the NBA Championship finals, where the Cavs were swept by the San Antonio Spurs.

In 2008, the Cavs ran into the Boston Celtics in the Eastern Conference semis, and lost in six games, but that year, James became the youngest player ever to score 10,000 career points. In 2008–09, James had an MVP season, and the Cavs had the best season in team history, winning 66 games and just their second division title. They also had the best record in the NBA. They swept the Pistons and Hawks in the playoffs, but ended up losing in the Eastern Conference finals to the Orlando Magic, 4–2.

The next year, once again James was MVP. Once again, the Cavs had the best record in the NBA. And once again, the Cavs failed to make the NBA finals. In fact, they didn't even make the Eastern Conference finals, losing 4–2 to the Celtics in the conference semis. The last game of the 2009–10 season in Cleveland—and James' last game as a Cavalier—was the worst beating the Cavs ever took in the postseason, a 120–88 loss to the Celtics.

The Decision

In 2006, James signed a contract with the Cavs that allowed him to become a free agent after the 2010 season. As the contract drew to a close, many teams flirted with him, and he seemed to treat them all just as coyly. He spoke of his admiration of Michael Jordan. Was this a sign he'd go to the Bulls? Akron was still his hometown. Maybe he'd stay in Cleveland. He had a certain level of reverence for Madison Square Garden. Perhaps he'd be a Knick. Jay-Z was one of his friends, and a part owner of the Nets. Could he end up in Brooklyn, by way of New Jersey?

Most Cavs fans, if they were honest with themselves, probably knew it was just as likely—if not *more* likely—that James was going to leave Cleveland as stay there. But when he announced that he would appear in a nationally televised hour-long special, hopes started to brighten in Cleveland. LeBron James wasn't just one of the most gifted athletes in the world; he was also a media-savvy marketer. He was far too self-aware and not enough of an egomaniac to call this TV special just to stick a finger in the eye of Cavs fans everywhere, right?

"I'm going to take my talents to South Beach and join the Miami Heat," he said in the special, which has come to be known as "The Decision."

"I feel like it's going to give me the best opportunity to win and to win for multiple years, and not only just to win in the regular season or just to win five games in a row or three games in a row, I want to be able to win championships. And I feel like I can compete down there."

James, Dwyane Wade and Chris Bosh were going to play together for the Heat. Wade and Bosh, like James, had signed contracts that would enable them to become free agents in 2010. And all three were teammates on the 2008 U.S. Olympic team, which won a gold medal.

The backlash, unsurprisingly, was enormous. Players like Michael Jordan, Larry Bird and Charles Barkley excoriated James for the move: they didn't want to play on the same team as their competitors; they wanted to *beat* their competitors. The New York media and fans were harsh in their judgments. The Cleveland media and fans were even harsher. The next day's *Plain Dealer* front page was dominated by a picture of James with the caption, "Seven years. No rings."

LeBron James' Salary Over the Years

Before James had even played a single game, he was already set to make millions of dollars in endorsement deals with companies such as McDonald's, Nike and Sprite. Even his salary with the Cavaliers during the 2009–10 season did not match the amount of money he makes endorsing products in his spare time.

Season	Team	Salary
2003–04	Cleveland	$4,018,920
2004–05	Cleveland	$4,320,360
2005–06	Cleveland	$4,621,800
2006–07	Cleveland	$5,828,090
2007–08	Cleveland	$13,041,250
2008–09	Cleveland	$14,410,581
2009–10	Cleveland	$15,779,912
2010–11	Miami	$14,500,000

Women's Professional Basketball

In 1996, the NBA Board of Governors announced the creation of a women's league, the WNBA. That year, Cleveland was named a charter member of the league, which would begin play with eight teams in 1997. It would be a summer league, so it wouldn't compete with the NBA.

The Cavaliers would run the team, called the Rockers, playing off Cleveland being the home of the Rock 'n' Roll Hall of Fame, which had opened two years earlier. The Rockers, whose logo included a guitar shaped like an *R*, had the same colors as the Cavaliers—blue, black and orange—with silver added.

At the same time, there was an American Basketball League (ABL), a women's league that had started in 1996 and had a larger share of quality players. The ABL featured a team in Columbus, the Quest, that won championships in 1997 and 1998. However, on December 22, 1998, the league was disbanded, leaving the women's professional basketball market entirely to the WNBA. Of the 50 players taken in the 1999 WNBA draft, 35 were former ABL players.

The Rockers made playoff appearances in 1998, 2000 and 2001, but never advanced out of the second round of the playoffs.

By 2000, the WNBA had doubled in size to 16 teams. The Rockers were part of the groundbreaking, but they went on to achieve another less celebrated first: they were the first WNBA team to fold. In 2003, owner Gordon Gund released his rights to the team, but no other buyer could be found. The team was then subject to a dispersal draft, where players were picked up by other teams.

Ohio Final Four

In the early 1960s, Ohio was the center of the college basketball universe. Ohio State won its only national title in basketball in 1960, beating California 75–55 at the Cow Palace in San Francisco.

The Buckeyes in the late 1950s and early 1960s were filled with talent, most of it homegrown. Larry Siegfried, a Shelby native, led the nation in scoring as a sophomore but ended up being overshadowed on his own team by two players a year younger: John Havlicek and Jerry Lucas.

Havlicek, a Bridgeport High School graduate, would go on to a Hall of Fame career with the Celtics after being a two-time All-American for the Buckeyes. While he was in Boston, he persuaded

Celtics owner Red Auerbach to take a chance on his former college teammate Siegfried, who was on the Cleveland Pipers when they folded.

Until LeBron James came along, Jerry Lucas was probably the best basketball player ever to come out of Ohio. Lucas led Middletown High School to back-to-back undefeated seasons, winning two state titles and runner-up for a third. He was a three-time All-American and the only man to win Big Ten Player of the Year for three straight years. Lucas still holds school records in field goal percentage (.624), rebounds (1411) and rebounding average for a season (17.8) and career (17.2). Lucas ended up playing professionally in Cincinnati (he was drafted by the Pipers but didn't play for them before they folded) and San Francisco before winning an NBA title with the New York Knicks. With that title, he had won titles in high school, college, the 1960 Olympics and the NBA.

One of the bench players for those Buckeyes teams was a Ravenna graduate named Bobby Knight, who wouldn't go on to play professional basketball but attained a lot of success as a coach, at West Point, Indiana and Texas Tech.

After winning the title in 1960, the Buckeyes went undefeated the next year, riding a 31-game winning streak into the NCAA Championship finals against Cincinnati in Kansas City. The Bearcats had graduated Oscar Robertson a year earlier, and so had switched their run-and-gun offense to a slower, control-oriented game. They couldn't stop Lucas in the finals, but they slowed the rest of the Buckeyes down enough for Ed Jucker, a Norwood native, to win a national championship in his first year as Cincinnati head coach. Lucas was named the tournament's Most Outstanding Player for the second year in a row.

People thought that the Bearcats' win over the Buckeyes was a fluke, but the two teams met again in the 1962 championship game—the only time the same two teams have met in the championship in back-to-back years. This time, there was no doubt. Cincinnati won 71–59 to clinch their second straight title, and the Bearcats' Paul Hogue, a two-time All-American center, was named Most Outstanding Player.

The Bearcats made it back to the NCAA Championship in 1963 but were denied a bid for what would have been an unprecedented third straight national title with a 60–58 loss to Loyola of Chicago.

All told, Ohio State—known more for its football than its basketball—has made 10 Final Four basketball appearances (one, in 1999, was vacated). They were runners-up to Oregon in the first NCAA Tournament in 1939 and to Florida in 2007, in addition to the two losses to the Bearcats.

The Bearcats, who had never even won a league title before Oscar Robertson's arrival, have made six Final Four appearances.

Ohio Basketball Facts

- The Cavaliers set a record on December 17, 1991, for the largest margin of victory with a 148–80 win over the Miami Heat.

- The Ohio State men's basketball team has made 10 Final Four appearances in the NCAA Tournament, exceeded only by North Carolina and UCLA, each with 18, Duke with 15, Kentucky with 14 and Kansas with 13.

- Xavier University is third all-time in NCAA Tournament appearances without advancing to the Final Four. The Musketeers have been invited to the dance 22 times, trailing BYU (26) and Missouri (24).

- The University of Cincinnati had the most picks in the history of the NBA territorial draft, with three: Oscar Robertson, Tom Thacker and George Wilson, all to the Cincinnati Royals. The Royals also drafted Jerry Lucas, from Ohio State University, as a territorial pick, since at the time, they were the only NBA team in Ohio.

Ohio Basketball Quotes

"I don't know how the Celtics can be so good. They don't even have cheerleaders."

—Ted Stepien, after the Cavs dropped the first game of the season to the Celtics in Boston Garden

"There is a lot of pressure put on me, but I don't put a lot of pressure on myself. I feel if I play my game, it will take care of itself."

–LeBron James

"I don't need too much. Glamour and all that stuff don't excite me. I am just glad I have the game of basketball in my life."

–LeBron James

"Man, meeting Michael Jordan for me was like… black Jesus walking towards me. It was overwhelming to me to finally meet the guy I've looked up to my whole life."

–LeBron James

Chapter 5

Boxing: Ohio Practitioners of the Sweet Science

The Fight of the Century

Every few years, boxing promoters, banking on people's short memories, will refer to a fight as the "fight of the century." One such fight came fairly early in the 20th century: July 4, 1919, at what is now Bayview Park in Toledo.

Jess Willard became the heavyweight champion of the world in 1915, becoming known as the "Great White Hope" in his fight against champion Jack Johnson. This 1919 fight would be his second official title defense, against the "Manassa Mauler," Jack Dempsey.

Willard was old for a heavyweight champion, at 37. But he was also one of the biggest men ever to wear the belt, at six feet, six inches. Dempsey was 24 years old. He gave up five inches and 60 pounds to Willard, but he had been fighting since he was a teenager, visiting saloons and saying, "I can't sing, I can't dance, but I can lick any SOB in this room."

It was a sweltering day in northwestern Ohio, with a thermometer at ringside reading 110°F. There were stands freshly built for more than 90,000 people—vendors were hawking newspapers for people to sit on so they wouldn't get any stain from the bleachers on their pants—including a section of the grandstand for women. But the actual attendance was estimated at only a little more than 19,000.

After one round in the fight, Dempsey looked tougher and stronger. He had knocked Willard down seven times. One overhand punch shattered Willard's cheekbone. Dempsey left the ring after the first round, thinking the fight was over.

But he was called back. Although Willard's face was swollen and one eye was shut, he answered the bell for the second round—and more punishment from Dempsey. Willard came out again for the third, before finally throwing in the towel before the fourth round. Dempsey was the heavyweight champion of the world. David slew Goliath.

The total gate was $452,224. That fight was the first of five Jack Dempsey bouts promoted by Tex Rickard, the founder of the NHL's New York Rangers and builder of the third incarnation of Madison Square Garden (the current home of the Rangers and Knicks is the fourth MSG) and the Boston Madison Square Garden (known as the Boston Garden). Rickard and Dempsey's next partnership, a Jersey City bout against Frenchman Georges Carpentier, was the first million-dollar boxing match, as well as the first fight to be broadcast over the radio.

Willard had two more fights in him, including a win over Floyd Johnson at brand-new Yankee Stadium in 1923, before retiring and working as a movie actor. Dempsey held on to the title until 1926, when he lost a decision to Gene Tunney in Philadelphia. The two men met a year later at Soldier Field in Chicago, and Tunney again outpointed Dempsey, who went on to open a successful restaurant on Broadway in New York City.

The Cincinnati Cobra

Ezzard Charles was born in Georgia but graduated from Cincinnati Woodward High School. He turned pro in 1940 as a middleweight, going 33–4–1 before World War II beckoned.

When he came back from the war, he was a light heavyweight. When Joe Louis retired as heavyweight champ in 1949, vacating the title, Charles beat "Jersey Joe" Walcott to claim the crown, and when Joe Louis challenged him a year later, Charles beat the "Brown Bomber" to hold on to the title. Charles lost the title to Walcott in 1951.

Charles is the only fighter ever to go the distance against Rocky Marciano, the only heavyweight champion to retire undefeated. They met again three months later, and Marciano won in eight rounds.

Charles, who has a street named for him in Cincinnati, retired with a record of 96–25–1. He died in 1975 from amyotrophic lateral sclerosis, more commonly called Lou Gehrig's disease.

The Man Who Took Down Sugar Ray

One of Ezzard Charles' title defenses was against a Cleveland native named Giuseppe Antonio Berardinelli, who took on a boxing name that reflected his machine-gun style of fighting: Joey Maxim.

Maxim fought Charles five times: twice before World War II and three times after. He lost all five. In 1950, he beat Freddie Mills of England to become world light heavyweight champion, a belt he held for two years before losing the first of three fights to Archie Moore. Maxim won fights over Jersey Joe Walcott and Floyd Patterson. And he was the only man ever to knock out Sugar Ray Robinson.

The two boxers met June 25, 1952, in front of a crowd of nearly 49,000 at Yankee Stadium. Robinson was beating Maxim badly, but he in turn was being battered by the heat. The temperature in the ring was estimated at 104°F, and referee Ruby Goldstein was felled after 10 rounds. Ray Miller stepped in to substitute. Maxim won the 12th round, and Robinson really started to wilt in the 13th. He couldn't answer the bell in the 14th and was carted to the locker room. He never fought in the light heavyweight division again.

Maxim, who died in 2001, finished with an 82–29–4 record.

Only in America

Don King was a Cleveland numbers runner and a convicted killer who ended up working for U.S. Representative Louis Stokes. He took a long shot and called Muhammad Ali to ask him for a benefit fight to keep some hospitals in Cleveland from closing. Ali agreed, the fight raised $80,000, and King's career as a boxing promoter was launched.

King's first triumph as a promoter was the "Rumble in the Jungle" between Ali and George Foreman in Zaire. Ali was promised $5 million, and the purse for the fight was $10 million. King also promoted the "Thrilla in Manila," where Ali met Joe Frazier in the Philippines.

In the 1970s, King promoted U.S. Boxing Championships in sites throughout the country, including the U.S. Naval Academy and Marion Correctional Institute in Ohio—the same place he served his sentence for homicide. Throughout the 1970s and 1980s, King promoted a who's-who of fighters: Larry Holmes, Roberto Duran, Julio Cesar Chavez, Evander Holyfield and Mike Tyson. "Iron Mike" later had little good to say about King, and the promoter has been in and out of court with Tyson and other boxers who have accused him of fraud. He once was asked by a Harvard Law student what his qualifications were to talk to the class. "I've been in more courtrooms than any of you," King replied.

Real-life Rocky

They called him the "Bayonne Bleeder," but for one night in Ohio, Chuck Wepner stood toe-to-toe with the greatest boxer of all time.

Wepner acquired his nickname after a bout with former heavyweight champ Sonny Liston. In what turned out to be Liston's last fight, he broke Wepner's nose and cheekbone. In all, Wepner estimated that he lost eight of his 14 losses because he was bleeding, and he has had more than 300 stitches in his face.

Wepner, a six-foot, five-inch, 225-pound journeyman who held the North American Boxing Association belt, took seven weeks off from his job as a salesman for Allied Beverage in New Jersey to go into training for a fight against Muhammad Ali. Wepner was angling for a shot against champion George Foreman, but Ali took the belt from Foreman in the Rumble in the Jungle—and then scheduled a fight with Wepner.

When asked if Wepner was a "Great White Hope," Ali said, "That's the only hope he's got."

The bout took place on March 23, 1975, at the new Richfield Coliseum. Wepner hung with Ali, and even knocked him down in the ninth round. Ali ended up winning the fight with a TKO in the 15th and final round, 19 seconds before the bell.

"There's not another human being in the world that can go 15 rounds like that," Ali said after the fight.

The fight inspired a young actor named Sylvester Stallone to write a script about a journeyman boxer who gets a title shot and loses, but goes the distance. Wepner was a consultant for the film, called *Rocky*. For his services, Wepner was offered $70,000 or one percent of the gross. Thinking that the movie would bomb, he took the flat fee.

Rocky came out in 1976 and shocked everyone, winning three Oscars—including Best Picture—and getting nominated for seven more. It has spawned five sequels, and the series has grossed more than $1 billion worldwide.

Wepner wasn't alone in his bad judgment; Don King, who promoted the fight, passed on backing the film.

Boom Boom Mancini

There wasn't a whole lot to be happy about in Youngstown in the late 1970s. The steel mills were closing down, throwing thousands of people out of work. The city was in its second mob war in a generation. Times were bleak.

But in 1979, a Youngstown boxer turned pro, and the area rallied behind Ray Mancini, who went on to become a lightweight champion and inspire a song by Warren Zevon.

Ray Mancini had the nickname "Boom Boom," just like his father, Lenny. Both men were lightweights. Lenny Mancini was angling for a title shot when he was drafted into the army in World War II.

He was injured in combat, and although he fought after the war, he was never the same fighter again, finally hanging up the gloves in 1947 with a record of 73–12–8.

Ray idolized his father, and from a young age, he knew he wanted to be a boxer. He put together a 43–7 record as an amateur, and turned pro. He won his first fight, against Phil Bowen, with a knockout in 1:59. He won his next 19 fights before getting knocked out by Alexis Arguello in the 14th round of a WBC lightweight title bout. Seven months later, Boom Boom knocked out Arturo Frias in the first round to become the champion.

On November 13, 1982, Boom Boom was to defend his title in a nationally televised outdoor fight at Caesar's Palace in Las Vegas against Duk Koo Kim, a Korean challenger. It was a brutal fight, and Boom Boom finally ended it with a technical knockout of Kim in the 14th round. But Kim never got up. He was transported to a hospital, where he slipped into a coma; he had a broken blood vessel in his brain. Doctors performed surgery, but Kim died four days later.

Mancini fought three more times, including an epic bout with Bobby Chacon, before losing his title in a 14-round fight to Livingston Bramble in 1984. He lost a rematch to Bramble and fought twice more after that, losing a 15-round split decision to Hector Camacho in 1989 and losing in seven rounds to Greg Haugen in 1992. Boom Boom retired with a 29–5 record, including 26 knockouts. He can still be seen in the Youngstown area from time to time, but he spends more time in California, where he works as an actor and producer.

Buster Douglas Does the Impossible

Columbus native James Douglas was a 42:1 long shot when he stepped into the ring against Mike Tyson on February 11, 1990, but he knew he could win.

The son of professional boxer William "Dynamite" Douglas, James grew up in the Windsor Terrace neighborhood of Columbus, where he attended Linden McKinley High School and threw himself into every sport possible. But boxing was in his blood, and from the moment he first stepped in the ring, it was apparent that he had inherited some of his father's talent in delivering a knockout punch.

Douglas entered into pro boxing in the early 1980s and quickly earned himself the nickname "Buster" for a devastating right hand that had the habit of knocking opponents senseless. He continued to make a name for himself through the 1980s, and by the end of the decade he had become somewhat of a legitimate candidate for the IBF heavyweight title.

In 1987, he fought Tony Tucker for the title, but because he lacked training and stamina, he suffered a technical knockout in the 10th round. Never one to take losing easily, Douglas devoted himself to his training and ended up notching six consecutive wins, including a knockout against Mike Williams that would earn him a shot at the heavyweight title against Mike Tyson.

For years, Mike Tyson had reigned supreme as the undisputed heavyweight champion of the world. His fighting style was vicious and explosive, and despite his relatively small stature for a heavyweight, he had amassed a record of 37–0 with 33 knockouts. In Tyson's fight just prior to meeting Douglas, he had knocked out Carl Williams in just 93 seconds. To say the odds were against Douglas would have been an understatement.

In the days leading up to the fight, Douglas suffered a major blow when his mother suddenly died after a major stroke. But instead of giving up, Douglas threw himself even harder into his training.

When the opening bell rang to signal the start of the fight, Douglas dominated early, using his 12-inch reach advantage to deliver powerful jabs to a surprised Tyson. Douglas managed to dance about the ring and continue his barrage of punches while Tyson refused to adapt his game to the much larger Douglas, instead trying to deliver his signature knockout power punch. Tyson managed to knock Douglas to the mat in the eighth round, but Douglas beat the count and continued on. Then in the 10th round, Douglas delivered a huge uppercut that had Tyson seeing stars, followed by a flurry of punches that sent Tyson to the canvas for the first time in his career. Tyson attempted to get up but could not beat the referee's count, and Douglas was named heavyweight champion, shocking the boxing world and making the few who bet on him very rich.

Despite the magnitude of his victory, Douglas' reign as heavyweight champion did not last. In his very next fight, against Evander Holyfield, he was knocked out in the third round and immediately after announced his retirement from boxing. Still, he will always be remembered in the annals of boxing as the man who took out the undefeatable Iron Mike Tyson.

Chapter 6

Golf: Hitting the Links in Ohio

The Golden Bear

The son of a pharmacist, Jack Nicklaus grew up in suburban Columbus. He graduated from Upper Arlington, a high school whose mascot became Nicklaus' nickname: the Golden Bear.

Nicklaus won five straight Ohio Junior titles, starting at age 12. While at Ohio State, he won two U.S. Amateur titles and an NCAA Championship, and mulled the next step in his career. A letter from golf legend Bobby Jones—who played for love of the game, not money—urged him to stay an amateur. Nicklaus wrote a letter to the USGA announcing his intention to turn pro, but vacillated about sending it. His wife Barbara eventually mailed the letter.

Nicklaus went on to become the best golfer of his day—and at this point, of any day. In 1960, he set a record that still stands; he shot a 282 at the U.S. Open, the lowest score by an amateur. In 1962, he won his first major, beating Arnold Palmer in a playoff at the U.S. Open. By the age of 26, he had completed a grand slam, winning each of golf's four majors: the U.S. and British opens, the Masters and the PGA Championship. All told, he has won each major at least three times. His total of 18 majors won—still a record—includes six Masters Tournaments, the last coming in 1986 at the age of 46; he is still the oldest Masters winner. That win at Augusta saw him fire a 30 on the back nine on the last day to roar back and win by one stroke over Greg Norman and Tom Kite. In 1998, at the age of 58, Nicklaus shot a five-under 283, still the lowest score at the Masters by a player over 50.

Nicklaus played a power golfing game, blowing the field out of the water at the 1965 Masters. His 271, then a record, gave him a nine-stroke win over Palmer and Gary Player, prompting Jones to say, "He plays a game with which I am not familiar."

Nicklaus started a second career while he was still golfing, as a course designer. It's estimated that he has designed or helped design 275 courses, and his company, Nicklaus Design, has designed a total of 346 courses, including Muirfield Village in Columbus, the site for the PGA's Memorial Tournament, run by Nicklaus.

He's also been given one of the highest honors that can be achieved in Columbus: he has dotted the *i* in the script "Ohio" that is done by the Ohio State University Marching Band.

Big Ben

Born in Columbus but raised in Ostrander, Ben Curtis had no choice really but to play golf as a youngster, given that his family ran the Mill Creek Golf Club. From the moment he could walk, he was swinging a golf club. Every chance he could get, Curtis was out on the course practicing. By the time he entered Buckeye Valley High School, he was one of the best in his age group and led the school golf team as their star. His skill on the greens continued into college life, as he was the leading golfer on the team at Kent State. It was one thing to be the big man on campus, but Curtis was by no means finished showing the world what he could do with a golf club.

Joining the amateur circuit, Curtis found instant success at the state level, winning the 1999 and 2000 Ohio Amateur Championship (the only other two golfers to win the Ohio Amateur in two consecutive years were John Cook and the legendary Arnold Palmer). After winning the Players Amateur in 2000, Curtis turned pro. Two years later, he finally finished high enough in the qualifying school rankings to earn a spot on the PGA Tour.

Curtis entered his first year on the tour with a lot of enthusiasm and hope, but things did not turn out so well for the rookie. He only once managed to crack the top 25 of any tournament. That lone bright spot came at the perfect time: at the Western Open in 2003, Curtis managed to finish a respectable 13th overall. Not a bad showing for the rookie, but most importantly, it qualified him for a spot in that year's British Open—one of the oldest and most respected golf tournaments in the world.

Odds against Curtis winning were very high, and he himself did not expect to beat a field of players that included Vijay Singh, Davis Love III and Tiger Woods. But as the tournament progressed, everything seemed to fall into place for Curtis. He birdied when he needed it and got a few lucky bounces. In the end, after sinking his final putt on the 18th hole on the final day, he won the tournament by one stroke. Not since Francis Ouimet at the 1913 U.S. Open had another golfer won the first major he played. The victory led to Curtis being named the PGA Tour Rookie of the Year for 2003. He has since won two other PGA Tour tournaments and continues to fight for the top spot. He currently lives in Stow.

Professional Golf in Ohio

Throughout the years, many professional golf events have been played in Ohio. The Buckeye State has been a stop on the PGA Tour continuously since 1954, starting with the Rubber City Open at Firestone Country Club. That tournament was held until 1960, when Firestone hosted the PGA Championship, and from 1961 to 1976, Firestone hosted the American Golf Classic. Firestone also hosted PGA Championships in 1966 and 1975.

Since 1976, the Memorial has been played at Jack Nicklaus' Muirfield Village in Columbus.

The Inverness Club in Toledo has hosted a variety of events, including two NCAA Championships, the U.S. Amateur, two Senior Opens, two PGA Championships and four U.S. Opens. The first

U.S. Open at Inverness took place shortly after the club opened, in 1920. The field for that open included an 18-year-old from Atlanta named Bobby Jones. But that Open was more remarkable for the fact that for the first time at a U.S. Open, the clubhouse at the host course was opened to the players. The players were so grateful that they chipped in and bought a grandfather clock, which remains in the clubhouse.

In 1931, Inverness was the site of what remains the longest running golf major. Billy Burke and George Von Elm were tied at 292 after 72 holes. At the time, the U.S. Open was a three-day tournament. The first two days were 18 holes apiece, and the third day was 36 holes. Then, as now, tiebreakers weren't settled with a sudden-death playoff, but with another round of 36 holes, played the next day. Von Elm sunk a birdie putt to pull into a tie with Burke, so they went out the next day to play another 36 holes. Burke won by one stroke. The two golfers had played 144 holes of golf in five days in a July heat wave. Von Elm lost 15 pounds in the heat. Burke, who went through 32 cigars during the tournament, gained three. After that tournament, the USGA decided that playoffs would be 18 holes, not 36.

Hale Irwin won the 1979 U.S. Open at Inverness, the last time the U.S. Open has come to Ohio. The last PGA Championship played in Ohio was in 1993, also at Inverness, and was won by Paul Azinger.

Canterbury Golf Club in Beachwood is one of two golf courses in America to have hosted the five rotating championships: the U.S. Open (in 1940 and 1946), the Senior Open (in 1996), the PGA Championship (in 1973), the Senior PGA Championship (in 2009) and the U.S. Amateur (in 1964 and 1979).

Scioto Country Club in Upper Arlington, where a young Jack Nicklaus learned the game, hosted a U.S. Open in 1926 (won by Jones), a Ryder Cup in 1931, a PGA Championship in 1950, a U.S. Amateur in 1968 and a Senior Open in 1986.

The last match-play PGA Championship was at Miami Valley Golf Club in Dayton in 1957. Also in Dayton are the NCR Country Club, which hosted the 1969 PGA Championship and the 2005 Senior Open, and the Moraine Country Club, where Byron Nelson won a PGA Championship in 1945.

Chapter 7

Potpourri: Pool, Fishing and the "Gravity Grand Prix"

Trailblazers in Ohio

The first black major league baseball player played in Ohio. More than 60 years before Jackie Robinson broke the modern Major League Baseball color barrier, Moses Fleetwood Walker played for the Toledo Blue Stockings in the American Association.

"Fleet" was a Mount Pleasant native and the son of a doctor. He went to college at Oberlin but transferred to the University of Michigan to play on the baseball team. He joined the Blue Stockings in 1883 when they were part of the Western Association. The next year, the team competed in the American Association, then a major league. Walker, a catcher, batted .263 in 42 games. A street outside of Fifth Third Field, home of the Toledo Mud Hens, is named for Walker.

He is one of several black Americans who were trailblazers in the field of sports in Ohio. In 1947, Jackie Robinson became the first black person to play in the MLB when he started playing for the Brooklyn Dodgers. Robinson was signed by baseball lifer and Ohio native Branch Rickey.

On July 3, 1947, the Cleveland Indians bought the contract of Negro Leagues player Larry Doby from the Newark Eagles, and Doby made his debut for the Indians two days later in Chicago. Doby also became one of the first Americans to play for a Japanese team in 1962. The Indians retired his number 14 in 1994, and he was inducted into the Baseball Hall of Fame in 1998.

The Indians made history again after the 1974 season, naming Frank Robinson as player/manager. The move had its controversy, because in naming Robinson, who came to the Indians in September 1974, the team had bypassed Doby. Robinson's first game as a manager was on April 8, 1975. The more than 56,000 fans who braved the near-freezing temperatures got to see Robinson, the second batter of the game for the Indians, hit a home run to help lead the Indians to a 5–3 win over the Yankees. The next year, Robinson led the Indians to their first winning season in eight years.

In 1946, when Paul Brown was assembling his football team, he signed two black players he knew from his days in Massillon and Columbus. Brown had coached Bill Willis at Ohio State, and while he was the Massillon High School coach, he coached against Marion Motley, a Canton McKinley graduate. Willis and Motley were the first two black players in the new All-American Football Conference, and among the first in professional football. The Los Angeles Rams, just relocated from Cleveland, had signed Kenny Washington and Woody Strode.

But in 1904, Charles Follis became the first black professional football player when he signed with the Shelby Athletic Club. Follis was born in Virginia, but his family moved to Wooster when he was two. His play in Wooster impressed Frank Schiffer, the organizer of the Shelby Athletic Club, and he lured Follis to play for Shelby, signing him to a contract in 1904. The Shelby team became a pro team in 1906, called the Blues. After that season, Follis, who was injured several times, turned his attention to baseball, swatting home runs for the Cuban Giants in Cleveland. He died in 1910 at the age of 31.

And in East Canton, William J. Powell became the first African American to design, build and own a golf course when he opened Clearview Golf Course in 1948. Powell went to Wilberforce College in Ohio and played in the first interracial college golf match, against Ohio Northern University at Lost Creek Country Club in Lima. After golfing in England during his time in the army in World War II, Powell came home to find many courses unavailable to him—so he built his own. The nine-hole course opened in 1948 and expanded to 18 holes 30 years later. In 2001, the course was recognized as an Ohio Historic Landmark and placed on the National Register of Historic Places. Bill Powell died on December 31, 2009.

The Gravity Grand Prix

In 1933, Myron Scott was a photographer at the *Dayton Daily News*. In the depths of the Great Depression, he found some teenage boys making their own cars and racing them down a hill. He told the boys to come back to the hill a week later, to bring some friends, and they'd have a race for a trophy.

A week later, 19 boys came back for the race. Scott then went to his bosses at the *Daily News* to see if they would be interested in sponsoring a bigger race, and on August 19, 1933, 362 boys participated in the race, with an estimated 40,000 spectators. The soap box derby was born.

Scott decided to do some advance promotion in other cities throughout Ohio and Indiana, and in 1934, 34 cities held soap box derbies to qualify kids to the first All-American Soap Box Derby in Dayton. Robert Turner of Muncie, Indiana, won.

The next year, Chevrolet signed on as a sponsor, and the derby moved to Akron, where it was run down Tallmadge Hill. The derby got a bit of surprise but not unwelcome publicity when Graham McNamee of NBC Radio, broadcasting from trackside, was struck by a derby driver and injured. He spent two weeks in the hospital with a concussion.

In 1936, a Works Progress Administration project built Derby Downs near the Rubber Bowl, home of the University of Akron football team. First prize for that year's All-American Soap Box Derby was a $2000 college scholarship. Second and third prize, of lesser value, was a Chevrolet. That year, the derby got its first international entrant.

The All-American Soap Box Derby drew celebrities, including actors Jimmy Stewart and Ronald Reagan, among its crowds of as many as 50,000 people. In 1972, Chevrolet ended its sponsorship of the derby, and the race limped along until Novar Electronics pledged its support in 1975. Novar continued as the prime sponsor until 1988.

In recent years, the derby has been plagued with financial problems, but the race continues to this day, every summer in Akron.

A Bad Day for Fishing

Every winter in the Great Lakes region, you hear about sport fishermen getting caught out on the ice. Sometimes these stories end in tragedy, but mostly, anglers are left red in the face as they try to explain to authorities why they went out onto the ice when conditions were unsafe. Rescue officials are used to planning extractions of one to 10 people at most, but on February 7, 2009, one of the largest ice fishing rescues occurred when hundreds of anglers made the ill-advised decision that morning to use a small plank of wood as a makeshift bridge to cross an open crack on Lake Erie to get to a better spot.

Fueled by the hope of a big catch, coffee and maybe a bit of booze, the anglers crossed the crack, not realizing that their added weight on the other side was increasing the size of the gap. It was a warm, sunny day, the type of day that would draw more than the usual number of people out fishing, but the ice over Lake Erie was a little softer than is safe. Also, a strong wind was blowing across the lake, causing a section of ice, on which the unfortunate group of anglers stood, to separate from the anchored shore ice, and the once six-foot gap suddenly became several hundred yards of open, frigid water.

Incredibly, the anglers didn't seem to notice. One said he wasn't aware of the problem until he started to see Coast Guard choppers. The fishermen just set out their gear, drilled holes in the ice and began to fish.

Calls to emergency workers started to come in around 10:45 AM about people trapped on the ice. Estimates of how many people were stuck on the ice ranged from 200 to 500. Local police and fire departments, and other river rescue units, as well as some volunteers, ferried people to safety by boat and helicopter, the largest helicopter rescue mission of people stranded on ice. Official reports said that 134 people were taken off the ice by rescuers and brought back to the mainland between Oak Harbor and Toledo. One fatality was reported—a man who fell into the water off a snowmobile. He was immediately pulled from the water but died at a local hospital later that day.

How did this happen to seemingly intelligent adults? The anglers were so determined to fish that common sense was pushed aside and a warped logic took over, allowing people to agree to build a bridge with planks of wood to cross a gap of freezing water to get to "better" fishing.

The Most Expensive Fishing Lure

Anyone who knows anything about fishing knows that it can sometimes get a little expensive: the rod, the boat and, yes, even the lures. Handmade specialty lures can run into the hundreds of dollars and are highly sought-after items by aficionados. But one lure in particular takes the cake as the most expensive piece of fishing tackle ever created: the Haskell Minnow. Riley Haskell of Painesville created this lure in the 1850s, and it fetched an incredible $101,200 at an auction on October 11, 2003. The South Carolina construction business owner and avid fisherman who purchased the lure set a new world record for the highest price ever shelled out for a single piece of fishing tackle.

The reasons for its high value are simply the style of the lure and its scarcity. Not much is known of Riley Haskell except for a few mentions at the patent office for his minnow design and on official documents. There is no evidence that he wanted to start a business with his lure patent, and he eventually stopped making them when the Civil War broke out and he turned his attention to making guns for the army. I wonder if anyone has tried fishing with one? At that price, it ought to catch the fish for you!

What's in a Name?

The most popular high school nickname in Ohio is the Tigers. Of the 828 member schools in the Ohio

High School Athletic Association, 36 of them are the Tigers (however, only one school, Cleveland Benedictine, uses the nickname Bengals; Cuyahoga Falls is the Black Tigers and Mansfield Senior is the Tygers). Panthers and Eagles are tied for second, with 35 schools apiece, and Wildcats are third with 33. But there are many unique nicknames in Ohio.

Some Catholic schools named for a member of the clergy use that member's title as a nickname. Cardinal Stritch in Oregon and Youngstown Cardinal Mooney are the Cardinals, while Zanesville Bishop Rosecrans is the Bishops.

Cleveland Glenville is the Tarblooders, a name that harkens back to workers on the railroad who covered stakes with tar before driving them into the ground. The tar would sometimes get on the workers' arms, burning them, so they looked like they were sweating blood. Former Tarblooders include Heisman Trophy winner Troy Smith, and Jerome Siegel and Joe Shuster, the creators of Superman.

Fremont Ross is the Little Giants, a name bestowed upon them admiringly by a rival. Sandusky players were quoted in newspaper accounts after a game saying that Ross played like little giants, and the nickname stuck.

The ceramic industry in Ohio provided two schools with their nicknames: Crooksville is the Ceramics, and East Liverpool is the Potters. Crooksville plays in the Muskingum Valley League, as does Philo, which has its own unique nickname: the Electrics.

Shenandoah High School in Noble County is named for the dirigible of the same name, which crashed in the county. Its teams are the Zeps.

There is a high school and law school in Cleveland named for former Chief Justice John Marshall. The high school's teams are the Lawyers. Marion Harding, named for President Warren Harding (Marion was his hometown), is the Presidents. But Warren Harding is the Raiders, a nickname they took after the consolidation of high schools in Warren in 1990. Harding was the Panthers, and Warren Western Reserve was the Raiders. Kent Roosevelt, named for Theodore, not Franklin, is the Rough Riders, and Taft High School in Cincinnati—named for Senator Bob, not President William Howard—is the Senators.

There are many teams that are the Irish or Fighting Irish, but other nationalities are represented too. Madeira's girls teams are the Amazons, Akron East is the Orientals, Sparta Highland is the Fighting Scots, Walnut Ridge is the Scots and Columbus Africentric is the Nubians.

A World Record

On March 19, 1954, pool legend Willie Mosconi was giving an exhibition at East High Billiards in Springfield. Mosconi, 40 at the time, was already regarded as the greatest pool player ever. By the time he died in 1993 at the age of 80, his name was nearly synonymous with the game he tried so hard to elevate.

Mosconi was a billiards child prodigy but fell away from the game as a youth. By the 1930s, though, he returned with a vengeance and went on to win 15 world championships. Mosconi retired from the professional circuit after a stroke in 1956 but continued to serve as an ambassador for the game, playing exhibitions and acting as technical adviser for movies, including *The Hustler*, in which he had a cameo.

When he went to East High Billiards for the 1954 exhibition, he played Earl Bruney, a local pool player. The two competitors played safe for a while, and Bruney pocketed the first three balls. Mosconi sank the next 200 to win the match. He then kept shooting on the eight-foot Brunswick table, breaking the record he set the previous fall of 365 balls pocketed without a miss, and ran it up to 526.

"I never did miss," Mosconi said later. "I just got tired and quit."

More than 20 people signed an affidavit, now in the Smithsonian, of Mosconi's achievement. The mark still hasn't been equaled, much less surpassed.

City of Champions

Although Pittsburgh laid claim to the name City of Champions, with titles in baseball and pro and college football throughout the 1970s, Cleveland could claim the same title in 1948.

That year began with the Barons winning the Calder Cup, the second out of five they would win under coach Bun Cook. That summer, the Indians won the American League pennant—after a one-game playoff with the Boston Red Sox—and beat the Boston Braves to win the World Series. And that fall, the Browns went 15–0 to win the All-American Football Conference.

In fact, on October 10, 1948, Municipal Stadium pulled double duty. That afternoon, a record 86,288 fans turned out to see the Indians and the Braves. Satchel Paige became the first black pitcher to appear in a World Series game, but Tribe fans were denied seeing the Indians clinch a World Series (they fell 11–6 to the Braves, and traveled to Boston to win the series in the sixth game). That evening, 31,187 fans came to the stadium to see the Browns beat the Brooklyn Dodgers, 30–17.

First in America

Crew Stadium is on the grounds of the Ohio Expo Center in Columbus. It has hosted high school football and soccer games, rugby games and concerts, but it was built for the Columbus Crew of Major League Soccer.

The Crew was one of the inaugural 10 MLS teams in 1996. They played their first three seasons at Ohio Stadium, the home field for the Ohio State football team. But when the Horseshoe was renovated, the Crew found themselves displaced. Ideas had been floated to build a stadium downtown or in Dublin, but both gained little traction. Then in 1998, the Ohio Expositions Commission approved a soccer-specific stadium—the first in the country—on the Ohio State Fairgrounds. The Crew opened the stadium in 1999 with a 2–0 win over the New England Revolution, before a crowd of more than 24,000 fans.

Chapter 8

Ohio Individuals: Immortals and Less Well-known Greats

Eddie Arcaro

Cincinnati native Eddie Arcaro was one of the best jockeys in the United States, winning more American Classic races than any other jockey in history and the only rider to have won the U.S. Triple Crown (the Kentucky Derby, the Preakness Stakes and the Belmont Stakes in the same year) twice.

Born in 1916 to a poor family, Arcaro could not take to sports such as football or baseball like many of the other boys in town did because of his small stature. Because of his size, his parents introduced him to horse racing, which he took to almost instantly.

Arcaro won his first Kentucky Derby in 1938 and would win the prestigious race four more times in his career. When he retired from racing in 1962, he had competed in 24,092 races, winning 4779, and earning more than $30 million in the process. He was inducted into the Racing Hall of Fame in 1958.

After he retired, Arcaro worked as a racing commentator for CBS and ABC and as a spokesman for Buick Motors. He died in 1997 at the age of 81.

Arcaro by the Numbers

Major race wins

- Jockey Club Gold Cup (10)
- Wood Memorial Stakes (9)
- Suburban Handicap (8)
- Preakness Stakes (6)
- Belmont Stakes (6)
- Kentucky Derby (5)
- Kentucky Oaks (4)

Racing awards

- United States Triple Crown (1941, 1948)
- United States Champion Jockey Award, by earnings (1940, 1942, 1948, 1950, 1952, 1958)
- George Woolf Memorial Jockey Award (1953)

Rob Dyrdek

Growing up in Kettering, Rob Dyrdek played the typical sports of an American youth, such as baseball and soccer, but he preferred something a little more challenging, with a little more edge.

He first picked up a skateboard at the age of 12 and immediately fell in love with skateboarding.

Within 30 days, he had already won his first competition and was signed on as a member of the G&S skateboard team. Rob threw himself completely into his sport, going as far as dropping out of high school in 1991 at the age of 16 to go professional and founding the legendary Ohio skate team Allen Workshop. That same year, he made his first skate film and began to receive the notoriety he had so craved.

After the film's initial success, Rob decided to make a drastic move. In 1994, he left Ohio, his home, for San Diego to make himself more visible to the skateboarding world. As his fame rose, Rob, as always, wanted to go big or go home.

In 2006, he signed on with MTV to star in the reality series *Rob & Big* with his best friend Chris "Big Black" Boykin. Always the entertainer, Rob showed off his skateboarding skills and used the show to set 21 Guinness World Records, including 46 consecutive front-side ollies, 12 360-degree kickflips in one minute, and 22 nollie kickflips in one minute. Today, he has a show of his own called *Rob Dyrdek's Fantasy Factory*, for which he and his staff produce all kinds of entertaining and wacky shenanigans to wow audiences.

Sarah Fisher

While her friends were playing soccer and talking about boys, Columbus native Sarah Fisher was watching NASCAR, Indy and Formula One races on television and envisioning herself one day speeding down the track.

As a little girl, Sarah spent weekends accompanying her parents Dave and Reba to the local tracks, where her father raced sprint cars. By the age of five, she pressured her parents to allow her to enter the midget races and go-karts, which she did until she was in her teens. Along the way she dominated her sport, winning the 1991, 1993 and 1994 World Karting Association Grand National Championships as well as the 1993 Circleville Points Championship.

At the age of 15, Sarah moved on to racing sprint cars, winning the 1995 Dirt Track Racing Rookie of the Year. However, the small cars and low speeds were not enough for the young racing phenom. With the support of her father, who was also her crew chief, the five-foot, three-inch blond started racing in the Auto Racing Club of America, the North American Auto Racing Series and the United States Auto Club, which allowed her to maintain a competitive schedule and helped her prepare for her eventual move into the professional realm.

In 1999, she hit another milestone when she became the youngest person ever to pass the Indy Racing League Rookie Test, a preliminary to entering the main Indy races. In 2000, she signed on to drive with Derrick Walker's IRL IndyCar Series team and ran eight races in the Indy Racing Northern Lights Series. In May 2000, she achieved a lifelong dream when she became just the third woman to compete in the Indianapolis 500. She did not finish the race because of an accident, but the experience was incredible for Fisher, who, at 20 years old, was also the youngest driver to race in the Indy 500.

She continued making waves in the racing world. At the 2002 Indianapolis 500, she became the fastest woman qualifier, averaging a speed of more than 229 miles per hour. In 2004, she made the jump to NASCAR when she joined the team led by Richard Childress. During her inaugural season, she scored four top-10 finishes, securing a 12th-place finish in the points standings, just out of the chase for the NASCAR Grand National Division West Series title. But after one year in NASCAR, she failed to find a new contract and returned to Indy racing.

Back at Indy, Fisher continued to race until the 2010 season. On November 29, 2010, she decided to retire from racing. She was only 30 years old, but she had spent 25 years racing.

William Elmer Harmon

William Harmon was born in Lebanon, Ohio, in 1862. He endured a hardscrabble childhood in the Oklahoma Territory (his father was an army officer), but as an adult, he made millions in real estate.

Harmon wanted to give back. He endowed a foundation patronizing African American artists, and he also distributed money for the establishment of parks and playgrounds, saying, "The gift of land is gift eternal."

There are many stadiums and parks through-out America that bear his name. In Fremont, Wapakoneta and Miamisburg, high school football games are still played at Harmon Field.

Harmon also gave land to his hometown that was turned into a five-hole golf course in 1912. The course was expanded to nine holes in 1920 and still operates today as Harmon Golf Club.

Nick Mileti

The alumni center on the campus of Bowling Green State University is named for Nick Mileti, a son of Sicilian immigrants, who attended the school. Mileti grew up in Cleveland, went to John Adams High School and after graduating from Bowling Green, returned to Cleveland and worked as a lawyer.

It was his connection to his alma mater that led him into Cleveland sports. He promoted a BGSU basketball game against Niagara at the Cleveland Arena. The game drew 11,000 people. It just so hap-pened that this was the late 1960s, when professional sports were booming—and expanding. And so Mileti tried to get into as many as he could.

He organized a group of investors to buy the Indians from Vernon Stouffer in 1972, outbidding a young shipbuilding scion from Cleveland named George Steinbrenner. Mileti said he needed to buy the team to keep it from moving elsewhere. There were already plans for the Indians to play 30 "home" games in New Orleans.

Mileti had started angling to bring professional basketball to Cleveland following the success of the BGSU game against Niagara. When the NBA expanded to Cleveland in 1970, he bought the Cavaliers.

He got into hockey when he bought the Cleveland Barons in 1968, and in 1972, he formed the Cleveland Crusaders.

In 1973, he helped get the World Football League off the ground and even bought a team, which he sold to another investment syndicate. The team became the Chicago Fire.

And in 1974, Mileti opened the Coliseum in Richfield, a small town between Cleveland and Akron. Costs spiraled to $30 million, thanks to rising interest rates and lawsuits from residents who didn't want it built in their backyard. Mileti could have built the arena—which served as home to the Crusaders, Barons and Cavaliers, as well as hosting concerts and other events—in Cleveland, but he saw the Richfield area as a potential regional draw. The Coliseum—a name that harkened back to his Roman roots—was within an hour's drive for five million people. Mileti sold regionalism.

Eventually, he sold the Cavaliers and Indians, and moved the Crusaders and Barons. But Mileti is still regarded as one of the people who saved major league baseball in Cleveland.

The Coliseum has gone the way of all flesh. The Gund brothers, George and Gordon, bought the Coliseum in 1981 and the Cavaliers in 1983.

In 1991, plans were announced for a new arena downtown, along with a new stadium for the Indians. The Coliseum's days were numbered. The Cavs moved into Gund Arena (now Quicken Loans Arena) in 1994, leaving the Coliseum without a tenant. It was demolished, and the land is now part of Cuyahoga National Park.

Jesse Owens

James Cleveland Owens was born in Alabama, but at the age of nine, he and his family moved to the city of his middle name. An error in record keeping led to his name of J.C. becoming Jesse.

Owens began setting records in track in junior high school. In high school at East Tech, he set world records, tying the mark in the 100-yard dash and setting a record in the long jump. He then went to Ohio State, where he won four NCAA gold medals in 1935 and four more in 1936. In the span of 45 minutes at the Big Ten track meet at the University of Michigan in 1935, Owens set three world records—in the long jump and the 220-yard dash and hurdles—and tied a fourth, in the 100-yard dash.

In 1936, Owens was part of the U.S. Olympic delegation to the Berlin Games. The games were a chance for German chancellor Adolf Hitler to show off his theories about the Aryan race and its superiority. Owens, a black man, shattered those theories, winning four gold medals: in the 100- and 200-meter dash, the 400-meter relay and the long jump.

He crushed German ideas of racial superiority, but he returned to America to find racism alive and well. He and his wife Ruth were turned away from hotels in New York City because of their race. "When I came back to my native country, I couldn't ride in the front of the bus," Owens said. "I had to go in the back door. I couldn't live where I wanted. Now what's the difference?"

Owens had a variety of jobs in his post-Olympic career. In 1976, President Gerald Ford awarded him the Presidential Medal of Freedom. In 1979, President Jimmy Carter gave him a Living Legend Award. Owens was named an Ambassador of Sport by President Dwight D. Eisenhower in 1955, and shortly before his death from lung cancer in 1980, Owens unsuccessfully lobbied Carter not to boycott the Summer Olympics in Moscow.

In 1990, Owens was posthumously awarded a Congressional Gold Medal, and in 2010, East Roadway in Cleveland was renamed Jesse Owens Way. The city high school track and field championships are also named for Owens, and Ohio State's home track—and the site for the high school state track meet—is Jesse Owens Stadium, which also serves as a home field for Ohio State soccer and lacrosse.

Lyn St. James

Born Evelyn Gene Cornwall in the Cleveland suburb of Willoughby during the postwar Baby Boom, Lyn St. James' first exposure to cars came through her mother, who drove a cab during World War II. Suffering from polio and unable to get around easily, Lyn got an appreciation of the freedom and independence the automobile could provide. Her father, who worked sheet metal at a local factory, instilled in her a love of machines and engines. Often, Lyn would be by his side on weekends, helping him with projects and getting her hands dirty. But when she was 17 and attended a drag race in Kentucky that a friend had entered, everything changed for Lyn.

Lyn's friend lost his race, and she teased him mercilessly about it. Annoyed, he suggested that she try her hand at drag racing. Never one to back down from a challenge, Lyn hopped behind the wheel of his Pontiac GTO and promptly won her race. She was hooked.

In 1970, she married John Carusso, who was also a lover of racing, and together, the couple raced in amateur competitions across the United States. In order to keep her own identity separate from that of her husband, she changed her professional name to Lyn St. James, and after dominating the amateur circuit in 1979, she turned pro with a historical run in the American International Motor Sports Association's Challenge Series, finishing second. Soon after, sponsors came knocking at her door, and in 1981 she joined the Ford Motor Company racing team. Over the next few years, she entered countless races and won numerous awards, but something still was missing from her racing career. She wanted to race in the Indy 500.

She was almost taken out of the professional circuit in 1991 after Ford dropped her from their ticket, but that did nothing to deter Lyn from her goal. She started her own racing business that same year, Lyn St. James Racing Inc. Just one year later, her hard work paid off when she made it to the Indianapolis 500 and heard the call: "Gentlemen, and lady, start your engines!" Although she finished in 11th place, she was still just the second woman in history (the first being Janet Guthrie in 1976) to start the event, and she did it at the age of 45. For her efforts, at the end of the season she was named the Indy 500 Rookie of the Year.

Over her career, Lyn St. James competed in 15 Indy races. She holds 31 international and national closed-circuit speed records, as well as two wins at the 24 Hours at Daytona marathon race. She gives back to her community with her charities and as a role model to other women all across the sporting world.

Tony Trabert

A Cincinnati native, Tony Trabert gave hints of his greatness when, in 1948, he became the first person to win three state titles in tennis in high school.

Trabert went on to win a singles title at the University of Cincinnati in 1951. In 1954, he helped the United States to win a Davis Cup. In 1955, he won the U.S. and French championships and

Wimbledon as an amateur. He won a total of five Grand Slam championships before turning pro in 1956. He retired from the professional ranks in 1963, but since then he has served as a Davis Cup team captain, was a television commentator for tennis matches, and was one of the charter inductees of the International Tennis Hall of Fame.

Dave Wottle

Dave Wottle, a Canton native, was inducted into the U.S. Track and Field Hall of Fame in 1982—five years after his hat.

Wottle graduated from Canton Lincoln High School, where he was turned from a sprinter to a distance runner, and he was considering going to nearby Mount Union College. But Bowling Green State University actively recruited him, and by the time he graduated in 1973, he had won two NCAA outdoor titles in the mile and held 13 Ohio records.

Wottle was at his peak for the 1972 Olympics in Munich. He was famously wearing his golf hat when he ran the 800-meter race at the Olympics. The hat was a tradition he'd started as a runner at BGSU, simply to keep the sweat out of his eyes. With 300 meters to go in the race, he was dead last. But he turned it on to pass the field and win the gold. The victory left Wottle in so much of a daze that he forgot to take his cap off on the podium!

Wottle briefly turned pro before serving as a track coach at Walsh College (1975–77) and

Bethany College (1977–81). He is currently dean of admissions at Rhodes College in Memphis.

Individual Sport Quotes

"Whenever I get to a low point, I go back to the basics. I ask myself, 'Why am I doing this?' It comes down to passion."

–Lyn St. James

"Once a guy starts wearing silk pajamas it's hard to get up early."

–Eddie Arcaro

Chapter 9

Ohio Hall of Famers

FOOTBALL

Pro Football

Ohio Natives in the Pro Football Hall of Fame

Each name is accompanied by the city or town in which the athlete was born.

Len Dawson (Alliance)
Dan Dierdorf (Canton)
Benny Friedman (Cleveland)
Lou Groza (Martins Ferry)
Wilbur "Pete" Henry (Mansfield)
Jack Lambert (Mantua)
Dante Lavelli (Hudson)
Dick LeBeau (London)
Tom Mack (Cleveland)
Chuck Noll (Cleveland)
Alan Page (Canton)
Don Shula (Grand River)
Roger Staubach (Cincinnati)

Paul Warfield (Warren)
Bill Willis (Canton)

Pro Football Hall of Famers who Played or Worked for the Cincinnati Bengals

Paul Brown
Charlie Joiner
Anthony Munoz

Pro Football Hall of Famers who Played or Worked for the Cleveland Browns

Doug Atkins
Jim Brown
Paul Brown
Willie Davis
Joe DeLamellieure
Len Ford
Frank Gatski
Otto Graham
Lou Groza
Gene Hickerson
Henry Jordan
Leroy Kelly
Dante Lavelli
Mike McCormack
Tommy McDonald
Bobby Mitchell
Marion Motley
Ozzie Newsome
Paul Warfield
Bill Willis

Pro Football Hall of Famers who Played or Worked for the Cleveland Rams

Dan Reeves
Bob Waterfield

Pro Football Hall of Famers who Played or Worked for the Portsmouth Spartans

Earl (Dutch) Clark

College Football

Ohio Natives in the College Football Hall of Fame—the Players

Each name is accompanied by the school for which the athlete played.

Cliff Battles (West Virginia Wesleyan)
Al Brosky (Illinois)
Bob Brown (Nebraska)
Dave Brown (Michigan)
Ross Browner (Notre Dame)
Ron Burton (Northwestern)
Jack Cannon (Notre Dame)
Bob Chappuis (Michigan)
Larry Csonka (Syracuse)
Tom Curtis (Michigan)
Harold Davis (Westminster)
Dan Dierdorf (Michigan)
Joe Donchess (Pittsburgh)
Bob Dove (Notre Dame)
Ray Eichenlaub (Notre Dame)
Benny Friedman (Michigan)

Bob Gain (Kentucky)
Ralph Guglielmi (Notre Dame)
Tom Hamilton (Navy)
Howard Harpster (Carnegie Tech)
Wilbur Henry (Washington & Jefferson)
Clarke Hinkle (Bucknell)
Desmond Howard (Michigan)
Cal Jones (Iowa)
Dick Kazmaier (Yale)
Jim Lynch (Notre Dame)
Jim Mandich (Michigan)
Jim Martin (Notre Dame)
Creighton Miller (Notre Dame)
Don Miller (Notre Dame)
Edgar Miller (Notre Dame)
Chet Moeller (Navy)
Ed Molinski (Tennessee)
Jim Moscrip (Stanford)
Alan Page (Notre Dame)
George Pfann (Cornell)
Jim Ritcher (North Carolina State)
Frank Sinkwich (Georgia)
Bill Sprackling (Brown)
Roger Staubach (Navy)
Herb Stein (Pittsburgh)
Harry Stuhldreher (Notre Dame)
Eddie Talboom (Wyoming)
John Tavener (Indiana)
Ernie Vick (Michigan)
Harry Wilson (Penn State, Army)
Lloyd Yoder (Carnegie Tech)

Ohio Coaches in the College Football Hall of Fame

Each name is accompanied by the school(s) for which the coach worked.

Harry Baujan (Dayton)
Earle Bruce (Ohio State)
Frank Cavanaugh (Cincinnati)
John Cooper (Ohio State)
Bill Edwards (Western Reserve, Wittenberg)
Sid Gillman (Miami, Cincinnati)
Ernie Godfrey (Wittenberg)
Woody Hayes (Denison, Miami, Ohio State)
John Heisman (Akron, Oberlin)
Paul Hoernemann (Heidelberg)
Lou Holtz (William and Mary, Arkansas,
    Notre Dame)
Don James (Kent)
Billy Joe (Central State)
Howard Jones (Ohio State)
George Little (Miami)
Don Nehlen (Bowling Green)
Ara Parseghian (Miami)
Doyt Perry (Bowling Green)
Bo Schembechler (Miami)
Francis Schmidt (Ohio State)
Ed Sherman (Muskingum)
Dick Strahm (Findlay)
Lee Tressel (Baldwin-Wallace)
John Wilce (Ohio State)
Fielding Yost (Ohio Wesleyan)

College Football Hall of Famers
who Played in Ohio

Each name is accompanied by the school for which the athlete played.

Warren Amling (Ohio State)
Bob Babich (Miami)
Jim Ballard (Mount Union)
Howard "Hopalong" Cassady (Ohio State)
Bill Cooper (Muskingum)
Jim Daniell (Ohio State)
Bob Ferguson (Ohio State)
Wes Fesler (Ohio State)
Randy Gradishar (Ohio State)
Charlie Green (Wittenberg)
Archie Griffin (Ohio State)
Merle Gulick (Toledo)
Chic Harley (Ohio State)
John Hicks (Ohio State)
Les Horvath (Ohio State)
Jim Houston (Ohio State)
Vic Janowicz (Ohio State)
Gomer Jones (Ohio State)
Rex Kern (Ohio State)
Mel Long (Toledo)
Jim Parker (Ohio State)
Chris Spielman (Ohio State)
Jim Stillwagon (Ohio State)
Gaylord Stinchcomb (Ohio State)
Jack Tatum (Ohio State)
Aurealius Thomas (Ohio State)

Bill Willis (Ohio State)
Gust Zarnas (Ohio State)

BASEBALL

Ohio Natives in the Baseball Hall of Fame

Each name is accompanied by the city or town in which the athlete was born.

Walter Alston (Venice)
Roger Bresnahan (Toledo)
Ray Brown (Alger)
Ed Delahanty (Cleveland)
Buck Ewing (Hoagland)
Rollie Fingers (Steubenville)
Elmer Flick (Bedford)
Jesse Haines (Clayton)
Miller Huggins (Cincinnati)
Ban Johnson (Norwalk)
Kenesaw M. Landis (Millville)
Rube Marquard (Cleveland)
Phil Niekro (Blaine)
Branch Rickey (Lucasville)
Mike Schmidt (Dayton)
George Sisler (Manchester)
King Solomon White (Bellaire)

Baseball Hall of Famers who Played or Worked for the Cincinnati Reds

Sparky Anderson, manager
Johnny Bench, catcher

Charles Comiskey (White Sox owner),
  first baseman
Buck Ewing, catcher
Jesse Haines, pitcher
Miller Huggins, second baseman
Ernie Lombardi, catcher
Larry MacPhail, owner
Rube Marquard, pitcher
Bill McKechnie, manager
Joe Morgan, second baseman
Tony Perez, first baseman
Eppa Rixey, pitcher
Frank Robinson, outfielder
Edd Roush, outfielder
Tom Seaver, pitcher

Baseball Hall of Famers who Played or Worked for the Cleveland Indians

Roberto Alomar, second baseman
Earl Averill, outfielder
Lou Boudreau, shortstop/manager
Jesse Burkett (Cleveland Spiders), outfielder
Stan Coveleski, pitcher
Larry Doby, outfielder
Bob Feller, pitcher
Elmer Flick, pitcher
Hank Greenberg, executive, owner
Addie Joss, pitcher
Napoleon Lajoie, infielder
Bob Lemon, pitcher
Al Lopez, manager
Eddie Murray, first baseman/designated hitter

Hal Newhouser, pitcher
Phil Niekro, pitcher
Satchel Paige, pitcher
Gaylord Perry, pitcher
Sam Rice, outfielder
Frank Robinson, outfielder and manager
Joe Sewell, shortstop
Tris Speaker, outfielder
Bill Veeck, owner
Early Wynn, pitcher

HOCKEY

Hockey Hall of Famers who Played or Worked in Cleveland

Each name is accompanied by the team with which the athlete is associated.

Andy Bathgate (Barons)
Johnny Bower (Barons)
Gerry Cheevers (Crusaders)
Bill Cook (Barons)
Bryan Hextall (Barons)
Reg Noble (Falcons)
Babe Pratt (Barons)
Nelson Stewart (Blues, Indians)

Hockey Hall of Famers who Played or Worked in Cincinnati

Each name is accompanied by the team with which the athlete is associated.

Michael Gartner (Stingers)

Harry Howell (Mohawks)
Buddy O'Connor (Mohawks)
Clinton Smith (Mohawks)

BASKETBALL

Ohio Natives in the Basketball Hall of Fame

Each name is accompanied by the city or town in which the athlete was born.

Gus Johnson (Akron)
Jerry Lucas (Middletown)
Nate Thurmond (Akron)

Basketball Hall of Famers who Played or Worked in Ohio

Each name is accompanied by the team(s) with which the athlete is associated.

Wayne Embry (Cincinnati Royals, player; Cleveland Cavaliers, executive)
Vic Hanson (Cleveland Rosenblums)
Jerry Lucas (Ohio State; Cincinnati Royals)
John McLendon (Cleveland Pipers)
Harold Olsen (Ohio State University)
Oscar Robertson (University of Cincinnati; Cincinnati Royals)
Lynn St. John (Ohio State University)
Nate Thurmond (Bowling Green State University; Cleveland Cavaliers)
Jack Twyman (University of Cincinnati; Cincinnati Royals)
Lenny Wilkens (Cleveland Cavaliers)

Notes on Sources

Books

Boyer, Mary Schmitt. *Browns Essential: Everything You Need to Know to be a Real Fan.* Chicago: Triumph Books, 2006.

—— *Indians Essential: Everything You Need to Know to be a Real Fan.* Chicago: Triumph Books, 2007.

Brinda, Greg, and Bill Livingston. *The Great Book of Cleveland Sports Lists.* Philadelphia: Running Press, 2008.

Cleveland Indians 2010 Information and Record Book. Cleveland: Cleveland Indians, 2010.

Creamer, Robert W. *Baseball in '41.* New York: Viking Penguin, 1991.

Dyer, R.A. *The Hustler and the Champ: Willie Mosconi, Minnesota Fats and the Rivalry that Defined Pool.* Guilford, CT: Lyons Press, 2007.

Feller, Bob, and Bill Gilbert. *Now Pitching, Bob Feller.* New York: Carol Publishing Group, 1990.

Golenbock, Peter. *Wild, High and Tight: The Life and Death of Billy Martin.* New York: St. Martin's Press, 1994.

Heisler, John. *Greatest Moments in Notre Dame Football History.* Chicago: Triumph Books, 2008.

James, LeBron, and Buzz Bissinger. *Shooting Stars.* New York: Penguin Press, 2009.

Kiczek, Gene. *Forgotten Glory: The Story of Cleveland Barons Hockey.* Cincinnati: Blueline Publications, 1994.

Levy, Bill. *Return to Glory: The Story of the Cleveland Browns.* Cleveland: World Publishing Company, 1965.

Menzer, Joe, and Burt Graeff. *Cavs: From Fitch to Fratello.* Urbana, IL: Sagamore Publishing, 1994.

Morgan, Jon. *Glory For Sale: Fans, Dollars and the New NFL.* Baltimore: Bancroft Press, 1997.

Moskowitz, Tobias J., and L. Jon Wertheim. *Scorecasting: The Hidden Influences Behind How Sports Are Played and Games Are Won.* New York: Random House, 2011.

O'Toole, Andrew. *Paul Brown: The Rise and Fall and Rise Again of Football's Most Innovative Coach.* Cincinnati: Clerisy Press, 2008.

Pluto, Terry. *Our Tribe.* New York: Simon & Schuster, 1999.

Rhodes, Greg, and John Erardi. *Big Red Dynasty: How Bob Howsam and Sparky Anderson Built the Big Red Machine.* Cincinnati: Road West Publishing, 1997.

Ross, Alan. *Browns Glory: For the Love of Ozzie, the Toe and Otto.* Nashville: Cumberland House, 2005.

Rudd, Irving, and Stan Fischler. *The Sporting Life.* New York: St. Martin's Press, 1990.

Sokolove, Michael Y. *Hustle: The Myth, Life and Lies of Pete Rose.* New York: Simon & Schuster, 1990.

Sowell, Mike. *The Pitch That Killed: Carl Mays, Ray Chapman and the Pennant Race of 1920*. New York: MacMillan, 1989.

Torry, Jack. *Endless Summers: The Fall and Rise of the Cleveland Indians*. South Bend, IN: Diamond Communications, 1995.

Newspapers

Akron Beacon-Journal

The Blade (Toledo)

The Cincinnati Enquirer

The Columbus Dispatch

Dayton Daily News

The Mansfield News-Journal

The News-Messenger (Fremont)

New York Daily News

The New York Times

The Plain Dealer (Cleveland)

The Vindicator (Youngstown)

The Wall Street Journal

Web Sources

www.baseballalmanac.comwww.baseballhall.org

www.basketball-plays-and-tips.com/lebron-james-quotes.html

www.bgsusports.com

www.si.com/vault

www.heisman.com

www.massillontigers.com

www.profootballhof.com

www.profootballresearchers.org

www.remarkableohio.org

J. Alexander Poulton

J. Alexander Poulton is a writer, photographer and genuine sports enthusiast. He's even willing to admit he has "called in sick" during the broadcasts of major sports events so that he can get in as much viewing as possible.

He has earned his BA in English literature and his graduate diploma in journalism, and has over 25 sports books to his credit, including books on hockey, soccer, golf and the Olympics.

Vince Guerrieri

Born and raised in Youngstown, Guerrieri is huge fan of the Browns and the Indians, and he tries to see a new major league ballpark every year. To date he has seen all but nine. He majored in both journalism and history, and chose journalism because he has an aptitude for writing and the knack for telling a good story. Vince is currently assistant editor for the Fremont *News-Messenger* and the Port Clinton *News Herald*, and his work has also appeared on MSNBC.com, USAToday.com and jjhuddle.com, as well as in *Cleveland's Best* and *Valley* magazines. The writing gig is perfect for him because, as he says, it beats getting a real job!